My Journey Through Life: An American Story

Recollections of the Family of Joe Henry Davis and Linda Craft

Gerald N. Davis

Five Sisters Publishing

Five Sisters Publishing
PO Box 217
Gretna VA 24557
www.5sisterspublishing.com

First Edition: October 2021
Published in North America by Five Sisters Publishing. For information, please contact Five Sisters Publishing c/o Anita McGee Royston, PO Box 217, Gretna, VA 24557.

Library of Congress Cataloguing-In-Publication Data
Library of Congress Control Number: 201993XXX
Dr. Gerald Davis
My Journey Through Life: An American Story by Dr. Gerald Davis/– 1st ed
p. cm.
ISBN – 13: 978-1-941859-84-1

1. SOCIAL SCIENCE / Ethnic Studies / African American Studies. 2. BIOGRAPHY & AUTOBIOGRAPHY / African American & Black see Cultural Heritage. 3. HISTORY / United States / 20th Century.

10 9 8 7 6 5 4 3 2 1

Comments about *My Journey Through Life: An American Story* and requests for additional copies, book club rates and author speaking appearances may be addressed to Dr. Gerald Davis, c/o Five Sisters Publishing, PO Box 217, Gretna VA, 24557, or you can send your comments and requests via e-mail to *gdavis700@yahoo.com*.

Also available as an eBook from Internet retailers and from Five Sisters Publishing.

Printed in the United States of America

Prologue

I began penning this memoir, autobiography, or life story a few years into my retirement from thirty-nine years as a student, teacher, advisor, and coach at an independent, co-educational boarding school in New England. If you are at all familiar with this type of secondary school environment, you may realize that it affords faculty very little time for writing anything other than progress reports and student grading, committee assignments, and conferences with students and parents.

In the summer of 2000, having just moved to Virginia, with no job for the first time in my adult years, I soon began to look for part time employment, as we had many things to do getting setup in our new home on the family property. In December, I was hired by a security firm and was assigned to a site here in Chatham. Ultimately, this allowed me time to do some writing, mainly letters to the editor of the local papers. Some of my associates, aware of my background, urged me to write my own autobiography. My usual response was to say that my life was too normal, without the drama necessary to attract readers.

I did begin, with my wife's help, researching my father's family history, here in PITTSYLVANIA County, Virginia. We found a lot of information, but only back to 1860s when my grandfather, Joe Henry Davis was born. There were several older extended Davis family relatives living nearby who offered interesting and valuable anecdotes, but much of this was hearsay.

My mother was still living here, and she could recall and verify some of these stories. Indeed, living on the Davis family homestead was a constant reminder of what my siblings and I and our children owed to those who were buried in the family cemetery on the hill behind our current home. However, both my wife Gale and I felt the need, or obligation, to extend our research to both of our parents' families. This soon became a daunting task, which was halted by Gale's illness.

Therefore, this memoir is dedicated to my wife Gale Reid Davis, who edited every line I wrote. She was a stickler for details and questioned my facts and generalizations. Although she is not here to see the final product, I hope she would approve.

To my father, George Nelson Davis, his brother Acie Richard Davis, and sisters, Queen Esther Early, and Sally Ramsey, I owe more than I can ever repay, for their hospitality and love.

My older brother Joseph Henry was always there to help me along my journey, as were my sisters Lorraine Davis, and Jo Ann Davis Wayne and my late brother George Dan.

However, throughout my life's story, it's my mother, Gertrude Minor Davis, whose love, nurturing, guidance, and generosity that rings true throughout the chapters of my life.

INTRODUCTION

by Gerald Davis

My Journey Through Life: An American Story, is my second autobiographical effort. As an 8th grader, I wrote *"My Life."* After seeing all my classmates reading my "book," which I printed on math paper, my English teacher, Richard Herrick, asked if he could read it over the weekend. Then he surprised me by typing it, without changing it in any way.

I have always enjoyed reading biographies and autobiographies, especially those describing the life and times of famous leaders. As a Hampton University student, I found Booker T. Washington's *"Up From Slavery"* informative, interesting, controversial and inspiring. But even more compelling was Frederick Douglass' *"Narrative of the Life of Frederick Douglass, An American Slave: Written by Himself,"* 1845. W. E. B. Dubois's *"Souls of Black Folk,"* 1903, also stands out as one the greatest American literary works. This anthology of essays dealing with the issues of Racism, politics, economics and the rivalry between himself and Dr. Washington is a "must read" for anyone who studies history.

In the modern era of the Civil Rights Movement, *"The Autobiography of Malcolm X,"* 1965, did much to heighten the sense of urgency among Americans of all ethnic groups. However, it took the publication of Alex Haley's *"Roots: The Saga of an American Family,"* 1974, to rejuvenate interest in Black family genealogy.

As a vital part of the American revisionist movement in African American history, "Roots" encouraged many Black families to convene annual reunions prompting hastily written family histories. The purpose of these published and unpublished scripts was to provide a valuable bridge to the past and honor the ordinary achievements of millions of hard-working Black families during our troubled past. The many facts, anecdotes, songs, family photos, and other memorabilia shared during these gatherings, provided new substance for books and pamphlets on thousands of families.

As African Americans, we come from a tradition which honors oral history. The "Griots" of Africa were important keepers and dispensers of clan and tribal history among Africa's non-literate cultures. *Roots* gave new meaning and value to the many stories passed down from generation to generation. It certainly made me aware of my own ignorance about my family's background, but I was too busy teaching, correcting student essays and tests to focus on my ancestry. I was, in fact, preoccupied with researching and writing my own doctoral dissertation. I should have spent more time asking my parents, aunts, and uncles about our family genealogy while they were able to remember.

Therefore, I have chosen to record my recollections of my family's background according to the years/times in which I learned of these individuals, facts, and stories. I must apologize for the gaps in the information and for my dependence on hearsay. Obviously, to expand the history of the family of Joe Henry Davis and Linda Craft requires input from many other relatives scattered throughout the country. I have also included information about my mother's family; but in both cases the data is sketchy.

FOREWORD

While the character of Gerald N. Davis was being molded as a child in Scotch Plains New Jersey, we were entering into two major wars on different continents, which would ultimately impact in a devastating way, the lives of most Americans. This was especially true with Americans of color. They were denied the right to fight for their country nor could they enjoy the rights of equal employment, housing and education. Exposure to these negative aspects of life can influence the development process of a youngster. Impressions are developing as are questions about the denial of freedoms empowered to whites. This along with a curiosity of history's past and a strong desire to learn, has helped guide Gerald into the teaching profession with emphasis on American History.

Gerald (Jerry as he is called) and I crossed paths in 1957, our freshman year, at what was then called Hampton Institute. Your freshman year in college is a time to become acquainted with new friends and set schedules and goals for what lay ahead. Even at that early point in our educational development, we both had ideas about what tools were needed to carry out our post-graduation missions. My goal was to become a chemist and work in a lab, developing new products that would advance science. Jerry's goal was far more personal and investigative. He believed a probe into history of the past could reveal answers to questions he had growing up, about the enslavement of Blacks, slavery in general as well as indentured servitude.

These issues were important to him because young Blacks growing up were being denied the truth behind the inequity of the races. He felt an obligation to right a wrong. He became a teacher of History.

After graduation Jerry chose to accept a two-year assignment to teach in Liberia Africa. He did this despite the many offers he received to teach in the United States. He wanted to teach the people of Africa while learning about the history of the beginning of slavery. What better way could you use the basic skills you learned at Hampton along with firsthand knowledge of Africa to carry back and teach Black Americans about a missing history. His two-year tenure in Liberia set up the beginning of his post-graduation studies leading to a doctorate in African and African American Education.

Thereafter Jerry fulfilled his dream as a college professor of history, of clarifying and correcting past inaccuracies about African Americans. He married, had two sons and continued through his retirement of reminding all of us of the importance of historical accuracy through his writings and newspaper commentaries. For all of the sixty years I have known Jerry, I can truly call him a visionary, who happens to be my friend.

Pomeroy M. Skeeter
IT Specialist Retired, USFDA

Acknowledgements

Anita Royston, *Five Sisters Publishing*
Publisher, Editor

Joslyn Gaines Vanderpool
Chief Editor, Co-Creator, *Brave Bold Beautiful Books*

Marcus McGee, *Pegasus Books*, *ContentConnect*
Editor, Publisher, Empowerment

Sterling Davis,
Book Cover Concept, *My Journey*

McCall Pomeroy Skeeter
Foreword

Table of Contents

Prologue

Introduction

Foreword

Acknowledgements

Appendix

Part One

My Parents, Siblings and Neighbors in Jerseyland

When I was a kid growing up in Scotch Plains, New Jersey, in the 1940s and '50s, I had little interest in my family's background. My parents never tried to keep us ignorant of our forebearers. Quite the contrary, Daddy and Momma both spoke fondly of their relatives back in Virginia. In fact, Daddy was quite adept at impersonating and mimicking those he remembered. He was so good at it that when I finally met some of my kinfolk in Chatham, Virginia, I knew who they were by the sound of their voices and accents. However, there was no organized and consistent effort or method to teach us our family history. Perhaps this was due to their own inadequate education, being distant from their family homesteads, and feelings of inadequacy or shame about situations they didn't want to share with us "chaps." In those days most southern black families didn't talk about serious matters in front of their children.

My earliest memories of my extended family on both Daddy's and Momma's sides involved stories of their childhood in rural Virginia. My father, George Nelson Davis, and my mother, Gertrude A. Minor, moved to Scotch Plains and Westfield, N.J. in the 1920s in order to continue their education and find employment. Daddy was living with his maternal aunt, Jenny Hardnett and her husband, Asa in Scotch Plains. Aunt Jenny was his mother, Linda Craft's sister.

Having exhausted the meager opportunities for schooling in Chatham, Virginia, my father was sent North to attend the non-segregated public schools in Scotch Plains. I believe both parents had to drop out at grade 7 or 8 in order to work and support themselves. The late 1920s and early 1930s were hard times, and I know Daddy was expected to send money back home to Chatham.

Momma was living with her aunt, Philly Wormly and her husband Robert in Westfield, NJ, where she attended the Roosevelt Junior High School. She was born in King and Queen County, Virginia to Florida Minor. Momma told us that a white man likely fathered her and a sister Ivory according to rumors in the small town of Cumnor. However, the man never admitted to being their father. Momma was only 5 years old when her mother died, resulting in the separation of her children. Momma was taken in by a cousin, and his wife, but she was subjected to cruel punishments, and her time with them was short. She was then rescued by Cousin Nancy Stewart and raised in Bordentown, N.J. until a teenager. She later moved to Westfield, N.J., living with her maternal Aunt Philly Wormly and her friend, Robert.

Aunt Jenny lived in the "colored" section of Scotch Plains, dubbed "Jerseyland." She was a devout Christian and member of St. John's Baptist Church which was located on Park Place just a few doors from Aunt Jenny's house. My parents met and married in this church, and my siblings and I practically grew up there.

Before my parents were married in the early 1930s, Daddy allegedly killed a Black man in Scotch Plains in self-defense. I say "allegedly" because he never talked about it. Nor did Mom. Such talk was not for kids' ears. My brother, Joe, and I learned of the incident from relatives of the victim and years later from our relatives.

Apparently, Daddy and a young lady from St. John's Church were walking across the Shady Rest Golf Course when they were surprised by a young man who knew the lady and was jealous. He emerged from the bushes and attacked my father with a knife before my father shot and killed him. I guess Daddy was aware of the threat and was armed. Afterward, he ran away to Uniontown, Pennsylvania, and back to Chatham.

Originally, I had the impression that Daddy spent time in prison, but my relatives assured me that he was never incarcerated, but he had hid out at home in Chatham until the incident was forgotten. The fact that he kept several guns around and did a little hunting lent credence to the rumors we heard about him. All I can say is that we were afraid to cross him and knew better than to handle his guns.

Like other men in the neighborhood, he would shoot his shotgun on New Year's and other occasions—one of which I remember, was of him shooting up through the trees to scare some kids who were trespassing at night. He yelled, "If you looking for the cemetery, you came to the right place!"

Daddy and Momma moved in with Aunt Jenny and Uncle Asa Hardnett in 1934, whose house (which also had a barn, where she kept her milking cow) was built by one Thomas Craft, a relative of Aunt Jenny. Our neighbors included all African American families who lived in homes they had bought or were paying for. I can only assume that Aunt Jenny and Uncle Asa had purchased their house, because I never heard her talk of a mortgage.

Aunt Jenny had a few shares of U.S. Steel stock, which Uncle Asa was given by a white family he worked for. This entitled her to a small quarterly dividend of $25.00 which was helpful at that time. Daddy worked in a factory in Garwood and paid the household bills; however, when Uncle Asa died in 1939, Daddy became the man of the household.

And when Aunt Jenny was no longer working as a domestic, she helped Mom with housekeeping and caring for me and Joe. But I remember her being in poor health, with high blood pressure and a serious nervous condition.

My older brother, Joseph Henry, was born in January 1935. Of course, he was named for his grandfather in Chatham. I was the second child, born in July 1938. Mom said she named me after a Jewish schoolmate who was friendly and kind toward her at Roosevelt Junior High in Westfield. I would have preferred "Frank or Bill," or something more masculine sounding. I shared **Dad's middle name**, Nelson. The twins George Dan, and Nancy Ann, were born in September 1943. Lorraine Mae was born in 1951, and Jo Ann in 1956. Although our parents spaced us nicely, Momma was always quite busy—too busy to work outside of the home, except for a few hours. She took care of a few kids for working mothers from time to time, so the house was always full.

Our house, or more correctly, **Aunt Jenny's** house, was crowded. There were 9 of us at one point sharing rooms and beds. There was little privacy, and we seldom all sat down together for meals. Indoor plumbing was late being installed, hence, well water had to be drawn and toted daily for drinking, cooking, bathing, and washing clothes. I had to draw two buckets of water before I went to school each day. Mrs. Grobes let us get water from her well, which was close to our house. Later, Daddy discovered a spring with fresh clean water, which we used until we had indoor plumbing installed.

We had a wood stove for cooking, located in the basement kitchen, and a furnace for heating, which required cutting, sawing, hauling, and stacking wood in the wood/coal bin. Joe would often tease me about getting the wood in before Daddy came home from work. We had an outhouse, hidden by the grape vines, which we used year-round, and Daddy insisted that we use it even in the winter.

We had to clear a path to the shanty. In the summer, it had to be cleaned out, and we had to help daddy with this nasty chore under the cover of darkness. In those days, soft toilet tissue was not always available. Usually, we used newspaper or whatever was within reach (like grape leaves). The only time I heard mom use a profanity was when one of us kids accidently knocked over the "shit pot." Looking back at this time always produced lots of laughs.

We were poor, but so were most of our neighbors. A few had indoor plumbing and other amenities like the Grobes', next door. Mrs. Elizabeth Grobes was the founder of the Jerseyland Park Community Center (JPCC) which was a 9-acre facility, owned by the people in the community. She was a wonderful neighbor who helped our family in many ways. She was the godmother for the twins and made them beautiful matching winter coats. She gave Joe and me our first paying jobs, doing chores around her house and at the community center and playground.

Mrs. Grobes had a daughter, Betty, who was a graduate of Wilberforce University and a competitive golfer. She hired us as her caddies and took me to several golf tournaments for black golfers in Philadelphia, Washington, D.C., and Cleveland, Ohio. These trips gave me the opportunity to meet many black professionals, doctors, lawyers, dentists, businessmen and women, as well as famous athletes like golfer Charlie Sifford and Teddy Rhodes. In Cleveland, we stayed with journalist, Simeon Booker, and his wife and baby daughter. I met the great boxer aka "The Brown Bomber," Joe Louis once, and he autographed my loud green hat that Bessy bought so that she could spot me in a crowd. She and her mother did so much to broaden my horizons and aspirations.

The Shady Rest Country Club was located in Jerseyland, just across the main street, Plainfield Avenue, which was the public service bus route. This club annually hosted the Negro National Golf and Tennis Tournaments. It only had a 9-hole course, and a tennis stadium with 3 clay courts. Our neighbors were one of its members, and as I became identified on the tour as her caddy, I got shout outs from many of the golfers wherever she played. They called me "Little Red" because of my hair and often paid me to shag practice balls. Wimbledon champ, Althea Gibson, played at Shady Rest, and I was one of the ball boys, which included local black male tennis professionals.

Daddy became a "special or auxiliary" policeman for the Scotch Plains Police Department. He mainly worked on the weekends or during special occasions and was responsible for maintaining law and order at Shady Rest and elsewhere in the community. Every weekend, there was a big dance with busloads of folks coming over from Newark and New York City. Occasionally, Daddy had to get tough with drunks and break up fights and brawls. He was always afraid someone he had disciplined would try to get their revenge by attacking us, so he barred us from hanging around the club. However, we snuck out and hung around the club anyway, as kids do. Sometimes we spied on couples having sex in cars in the parking lot.

Having Fun, Creating Mischief and Learning to Work

Dad's attitude on raising children was to keep us busy helping with the daily chores. He believed in two-thirds work and one-thirds play. Yet I can honestly say that I had a normal childhood of fun and play as well as work. We lived close to the woods and spent many hours climbing trees, riding the young, slender ones to the ground so beautifully described in the poem, "Birches," by Robert Frost. We built huts in trees, spent overnights there, and cooked meals around campfires. We sometimes incurred the wrath of our mothers, whose pantries we raided for onions, potatoes and other ingredients.

Picking huckleberries, blackberries, and selling some to neighbors who baked dumplings and pies was especially rewarding. Some neighbors had fruit trees, loaded with cherries, apples and pears, which we often helped ourselves to under the cover of darkness. We often helped ourselves to the neighbor's tomatoes and even brought our own saltshakers from home to enhance the flavor of the fruit. Occasionally in our nocturnal gorging, we became hilarious and boisterous and hence were discovered and forced to jump and run, which sometimes resulted in injuries. These moonlight adventures were not without danger, and sometimes even punishment at home.

Given to mischief, as were most of my buddies, these pranks were not limited to the Halloween season. The Shady Rest Country Club and its 9-hole golf course and 3 clay tennis courts were often our victims. Mr. Willis, the owner/manager of the facility, was not popular among the youth of Jerseyland, because he seldom allowed us to play golf or tennis. We were used as caddies and ball boys, but not offered lessons ourselves. Hence, we sometimes wreaked havoc on the greens, or in the clubhouse. Nothing major, mind you, but enough to warrant severe consequences if caught.

Our antics included taking the old rickety work truck used to carry mowers and tools from its shed, driving across the course at night and leaving it in the woods, far from the clubhouse. Some of the older guys would climb up the lattice at the club house and peek in on the ladies' powder room and bathroom. Other guys would deflate the tires on cars at the club or place chairs in front or behind cars parked in the lot and then hide in the bushes, waiting for the drivers to discover the prank.

One memorable incident involved my father and my friend, *"Slick," as he was called, during a tennis tournament. Slick was sitting in the bleachers, watching the match, when Dad walked by on patrol in full uniform and was shot in the face by Skeeta's water pistol. Dad's reaction was swift; he reached up through the seats and pulled Skeeta down, inflicting a few scratches and lots of embarrassment. We have often laughed about this over the years.

One evening, we almost lost our lives at the hands of Mr. Jenkins, an older gentleman, and a neighbor on Park Place, who spent hours in his garage, working on his car. Known to react swiftly to kids' pranks, my two buddies and I were on the hill at Jimmy Hamlett's dump, throwing cans and bottles, when one friend suggested we take aim at Jenkins's garage. Afterward, we ran away from the scene, laughing hysterically, until we met a local wino, with whom we foolishly shared our prank. Looking for money to buy wine, he threatened to tell Mr. Jenkins, unless we gave him 50 cents, which we couldn't come up with. So he made good on his threat, and hence, Pop Jenkins waited for us to come home.

Armed with a double barrel shot gun, Mr. Jenkins was furious. Tears streamed down his cheeks as he held his gun—cocked, loaded, and pointed stealthily in our direction—trapping us against a wall. He stated in no uncertain terms he would "wash us away." Scared stiff, we apologized profusely and promised never to do it again, but Jenkins was not impressed. Fortunately, a neighbor who heard the commotion arrived and begged Mr. Jenkins to spare our lives. He eventually yielded, lowered the gun and let us go. Daddy was waiting for me and threatened a severe thrashing when I got home. But fortunately, my Aunt Sally and Uncle Shirley were visiting, and I escaped the whipping.

Despite the near life-ending encounter with Mr. Jenkins, there were other instances of mischief. One of our most daring acts was the night we decided to use a devil's mask and knocked on doors to see folks' reactions. I don't know whose idea this was, but one guy supplied the rubbery red and black mask, another one brought his father's old overcoat, and one boy contributed a pair of big boots. The first house we approached was in the black neighborhood referred to as "The Big Woods," which was located between Jerseyland and Westfield.

Our first victim, Mrs. Bullock, who upon hearing the knock on her door said, "Come on in," probably expecting a next-door neighbor. When she opened the door, she saw this hideous figure wearing a grotesque mask, and began screaming.

"Lord, I done seen the Devil!"

We ran away laughing and looking for the next house to approach. One lady simply slammed the door shut after facing our "devil," the tallest guy in the gang.

After word circulated in the neighborhood, we decided to approach one more house. This was the Bennett family, and after one of the daughters screamed and slammed the door, her father came out with his shotgun and blasted through the treetops as we ran off laughing. By this time, we were exhausted and frightened, but one guy insisted on trying another house. This time it was the Kates's home on Plainfield Avenue, but as luck would have it, their son, who was in his twenties, answered the door and grabbed our buddy with the devil's mask and exposed him as the rest of us ran across the golf course. Fortunately for me, my father didn't hear about this until the furor subsided.

I spent a lot of time with the Harold Craft family, who lived next door to Mr. Jenkins. The father was also an auxiliary policeman, but he worked as a chef in Elizabeth or Newark. His son was a year older than me, as were his 2 sisters. One day, while I was teasing one of the sisters and being a total nuisance, their father, who was sleeping upstairs, came down and handcuffed me to the bed. He went off somewhere and left me for at least 3 hours to think about the error of my ways. The family later moved to Keyport, N.J. where on occasion I visited them, but we eventually lost touch over the years.

Playing paddle tennis on the asphalt pavement of Morse Avenue in front of our house was one of our favorite activities. We made the paddles from the wooden fruit crates that we scavenged from Hamletts' dump. He also owned and operated a garbage/trash disposal business and allowed us to use the old crates on his property. We actually marked lines on the road with chalk (and once with paint) to divide the service courts. When cars approached, we stopped and let them pass, but occasionally, in our enthusiasm, we tried the patience of some drivers who honked their horns in frustration. One such example was Dr. Thompson, a local black physician, who was on his way to a see a patient. He later told Daddy about how I was one of the kids who made him late for a house call.

Personal Watershed Experiences, Maturing

I learned to swim the hard way. One day, at a swimming hole, I was thrown off the bridge into water 5 or 6-feet deep by Whitmore Stewart. I somehow swam to the other bank, surprising and delighting myself. From that day on, I embraced every opportunity to go swimming. One of our favorite holes was Twin Falls in Scotch Plains, across Highway 22, up behind Weldon's construction site. The depth was at least 10 feet in one spot, but there were shallow places of only 3 feet. I remember the thrill of diving down into the deep water, but I was frightened by the coldness and pressure in my desperate attempt to return to the surface. This site was at least 4 or 5 miles from home.

My mother was not happy about my swimming at dangerous sites. After one boy was severely injured during a dive, I never returned.

However, there was no local swimming pool in the Jerseyland Park Community Center, so we had to resort to whatever opportunities and places we could find, including creeks and ponds, and on one occasion even the golf course, which had a shallow pool of rainwater. While wading across it one afternoon, I got a deep cut on my knee. I then began using the public pool in Rahway Township, which required a 10-mile bus ride, and on one occasion produced an incident that influenced my attitude toward policemen.

When I was returning from Rahway pool one day, I was questioned by a policeman in Westfield on Elm Street. When I got off the bus on Central Avenue, I had to catch another bus to get home, and I took a shortcut through an alley to reach the other bus stop when the officer approached me.

"What are you doing coming out of the alley? Show me your ID?" Surprised by his question and his hostile manner, I challenged him.

"Why are you picking on me, when many people use that alley?" He took his nightstick and pushed me against the wall.

"Show me your ID, or I'll take you to the police station!" I swallowed my pride and offered him my identification card. "Next time an officer asks you for this, don't be such a smartass," he said and walked off.

The incident had a profound effect on me, but fortunately, Mrs. Grobes used every opportunity to involve local kids in constructive activities at the community center and its playground. She taught knitting, basket-weaving, sewing and other skills for the girls, and she gave the boys lessons in carpentry, masonry and the use of various lawn and garden tools. She had great plans for clearing the 9 acres and making a tennis court and additional buildings for indoor functions. As one of her main helpers, I recall using the new bush knife tool to clear a spot behind one of the neighbors' property. She brought out hotdogs and a few condiments and we roasted the wieners using fresh cut forks from bushes as skewers. Sitting around the fire and enjoying that treat was so pleasing.

On snowy days, Mrs. Grobes would open the center and fire up the potbellied stove and prepare hot chocolate for us as we came in from the hills across the street. Her homemade donuts were a special treat on those cold nights. Some kids came in from sledding with bruises and scratches, and Mrs. Grobes was ready with iodine and band-aids. Whenever an argument turned physical, she would stop the pugilists, using the moment as an opportunity to teach us how to peacefully settle disputes.

Shaping of a Scholar

I consider myself fortunate to have two loving parents and an aunt who did much to steer me in the right direction, despite my tendency to give into peer pressure at times. Daddy was the tough disciplinarian, ready with the switch or whatever was handy at the moment. Mom was the best listener and comforter when no one else understood.

She and Dad would disagree and argue sometimes, but I never heard them use profanity or strike one another. Mom may not have agreed with Dad's decision on what we could or could not do, but she wouldn't contradict him in our presence. If he was applying the switch or belt too much, she and Aunt Jenny would intervene, like the time he was whaling away on Joe for some infraction.

The one time I can clearly remember when my father disciplined me was outside, while I was helping him move some boards. I was wearing a new colorful sweater I had purchased, and Daddy said, "You should have on some old work shirt," to which I foolishly replied, "I bought the sweater myself," implying that it wasn't his concern. In the next instant, Daddy took one of the pine slabs he pulled off the truck and hit me flat across the chest, knocking me down. Then he stood over me with the slab, threatening to strike me again, but I pleaded for mercy and apologized. That was the last time he had to strike or discipline me. I learned my lesson.

I spent a lot of hours with my dad, cutting down trees and sawing up the wood we used at home. My first job as a little kid, aged 9 or 10 years old, was to chop up the twigs into a big pile of kindling with my own hatchet. As I got older, I helped Dad with the 6-foot crosscut saw, downing big trees. He would climb the tree and cut the big limbs and tie a rope up high, which would help us fell the tree in the safe direction, using the truck to increase the tension on the rope. He was careful to avoid accidents and constantly cautioned me about taking chances, like swinging the maul without watching for overhead limbs or clothes lines.

The most dangerous aspect of our work was using the saw he powered with a 3-inch belt, wrapped around the rear truck tire. He would guide the log on the saw bench, and I would catch the chunk of wood and throw it on the pile. The saw made such a loud whine that neighbors would stop by to watch and comment.

Since my dad owned a truck, he moved furniture for neighbors and got various tree surgeon jobs. One lady hired him to cut down and remove this big oak tree, and later asked us to paint her house. Working with him at these sites taught me valuable lessons about how to conduct myself around other adults and about how to earn money in my after-school hours.

During those times, I was often angry for having to work instead of hanging with friends, but years later, I realized the importance of these hours I spent working with Dad. He was adept at defusing my anger on these jobs by telling stories and jokes until I forgot about where I'd rather be. One of his favorites was describing one neighbor's preference for putting the wedge right on the knot when splitting a log.

I was always interested in carpentry and jumped at every opportunity to learn the skills of the trade. Helping Mrs. Grobes build her cement block shed next door was instructive and fun. When Mr. Bill Fowler was building his new house on Hamlett's place, I helped put in the floorboards. There was no plywood, wafer board or nail guns at that time, so we had to do a lot of nailing with hammers.

Mr. Porte was doing the masonry work, and I helped him with mixing the mortar and toting the cinder blocks. Mr. Fowler gave me a few dollars, but I was mainly volunteering. He would not let me help with the roof or do any dangerous tasks.

At home, I did various repairs on the front porch and stairs, putting up screens, so we could sit or sleep out there in the evenings. At the JPCC, I helped build and repair the sheds that held the tools and equipment. Amelia Casey and I painted the Community Center House, and Mrs. Grobes taught me how to use oil or grease on the nail when the board was tough.

Like most teens, my first money earning opportunities involved cutting lawns and doing light yard work for neighbors. I remember starting a Christmas Club savings account with my first real earnings from working for Mrs. Grobes and other neighbors. Daddy paid me a few bucks after some jobs, and he usually urged me to save some of it for a rainy day. But my first regular paycheck came from delivering newspapers.

I worked for Mr. Hall and his wife, Louise, who owned and operated a newspaper delivery service in Scotch Plains. I can't recall when I got my first paper route, but I was at least 14 or 15, and strong enough to handle a stack of papers on my bicycle. My daily route was along Westfield Road in Scotch Plains, where new houses were being constructed. Years later, the new Scotch Plains High School was built in this area. Rain, or shine, snow or sleet, I made my deliveries; sometimes I had to walk, due to a flat tire or other problems.

I learned how to deal with cranky and difficult customers. One lady insisted that I put her paper inside the storm door at the back of her house, which required me to get off my bike. She complained about me riding across her lawn, and Mr. Hall told me something I later repeated to kids who work with me: *The customer is always right. They pay your salary and mine, so grin and bear their complaints.* At one house, a young white boy asked me if I was a "nigger," and when I got off my bike to react, he ran inside. I told Mr. Hall, but I don't know what he did about it.

Most of the customers were nice. I worked the early morning delivery routes on weekends, delivering the *New York Times,* the *Herald Tribune, Philadelphia Inquirer* and the *Newark Star Ledger.* I stood on the running board of a 1940 Buick 4-door sedan with my head inside the back window until I was dropped off with the papers for a street or cul-de-sac. Taking the most convenient route or path across the lawns, I would meet the driver and the other runner at another street. During the winter months, it was usually very cold, so we had to dress accordingly. When we finished, the driver would stop by the Park Avenue Bakery, and we would buy pastries before being driven home.

When I got my driving license, I worked in the afternoons as well as the weekends. Our high school was on a half-day schedule, so I was free to work every afternoon. The Halls were pleased with my work and kept the job open for me during vacations when I went to college. On Saturday mornings at 3p.m., I helped them sub, or I put the various sections of the papers together in their garage. This job of driving the van with one or two younger boys on board forced me to be a safer driver, especially in the winter, when the roads were slippery with ice and snow.

When I went to college, I continued working for the Halls, but I found other part-time employment at a funeral home, doing odd jobs for a family in Westfield. I also worked in a foundry, delivering and setting up above-ground swimming pools, and at a window shade and venetian blind shop. I learned valuable skills and work habits at these sites, but I only stayed a short time at most of them. Daddy advised me to take the first job I was offered and continue searching for a better one. I was generally able to find a part-time job near home.

I had worked at a steel company during the previous summer, earning union wages and time-and-a-half for overtime. An employee who lived on New York Avenue and who knew Dad got me the job, claiming I was his relative and a college student. He said, "If the white guys got summer jobs for their kids, why not you?"

During my tenure, I learned the way a union shop operated and how to get along with the fulltime employees. There was an old Black guy in charge of the furnace, who I sometimes had lunch with. "Don't get comfortable here because of the wages. Continue with your education and become somebody. Avoid the BS talk in the canteen and carry yourself with dignity. Don't act the fool like some of these clowns expect you to because you Black," he warned. I valued and followed this man's counsel and have thought about him and others who helped me along my journey.

As a non-union summer employee, I had no permanent job, but I was assigned to different departments by the foreman. I learned the art of "feather-bedding" while testing steel pipes underwater for leaks. As I got familiar with this task, I was able to do at least 70-85 per hour, but another union employee told me to only test 50 per hour and then take a break. So I went along and got along, following the union's policy. They paid me $2.90 an hour, and over $3.00 on second shift. At the foundry, I only earned $1.85.

PERSONAL WATERSHED EXPERIENCES
PLANNING FOR THE FUTURE

When I think about my teenage years and the seminal experiences that influenced the important decisions I made—peer pressure, church activities and parental guidance come to mind. As a light-skinned "colored" boy, with reddish brown curly hair, early on I became sensitive about looks. Most of my friends were of a darker hue with wooly, coarse, or kinky hair. They would tell me, "You got that good hair," when we were swimming or in the showers at school.

My brother Joe and I sometimes were told that we looked more like the "gray boys" in Crestwood, which always got an immediate and strong reaction from us. We rejected any notion that we were not authentic black kids, like our friends. We did much to go along to get along. Our best friends had dark complexions, like the majority of the neighborhood kids, and like them, we fought with any white kid who used the epithet, "nigger."

I cringe in shame when I think of the many times I heard black guys tease others because they were very dark, or had thick lips, wide nostrils or nappy hair. My mother taught us to never do such, because people can't help the way they look, and that it had nothing to do with their character. I may not have initiated such teasing, but I'm sure I laughed like everyone else. One example comes to mind about the time a white kid we passed on our way to school was pressured to agree or disagree that a dark-skinned guy was really Black. No matter what answer he gave, he was toast.

Playing at night, black guys were told to open their eyes and show their teeth so they could be seen. Most of this teasing was not mean-spirited, but it revealed how deep our sense of inferiority and shame was. When referring to a Black person back then, the polite label whites and Blacks used was "colored or Negro." Most Blacks were not ready at that time to accept "African American" or "Black," because we had been taught that Africans were savages and backward by "Tarzan" movies and the American media publications.

I had girlfriends at age 10, but we only kissed and hugged and held hands. I used to play "house" with a girl in her aunt's shed. Her older brother and sister were usually home at these times and came out to tease us. As I experienced puberty, my sexual experiences were more serious, usually with more privacy. Some girls enjoyed or allowed the necking, fondling, and probing—up to a point, and sometimes beyond. *The Ford girls, who lived two doors away, allowed me some liberties, and the Kemps' daughters were usually entertaining when their parents were out.

Both the neighborhood girls and boys found opportunities to test the limits of sexual experimentation, mindful of parental guidelines and warnings. When word of a teen pregnancy spread, parents and guardians became stricter and more vigilant. Daddy often warned me about the danger of getting a girl pregnant, which he viewed as a roadblock for future success. The stigma on teen pregnancy was very formidable then, and there were a few examples of local girls with babies for reference.

I'm sure that Daddy's constant warnings helped me avoid this mistake. There was peer pressure to show your sexual prowess and masculinity. I would often hear older guys or grown men bragging about the number of girls or women they had bedded or impregnated. There was also teasing or ridiculing for a guy whose girlfriend or woman reported his inability to perform or satisfy.

I enjoyed going to the dances and social gatherings at the community center, and parties at neighborhood homes. I was not a naturally gifted dancer. I was too self-conscious and lacked the confidence to perform properly on the dance floor. However, I would get up and look for a partner to slow grind to *Earth Angel*, the popular song at the time. I was sensitive about my height, and the girls seemed taller and much better dancers.

In our house—no dancing, card-playing, or games akin to gambling were allowed. Since Aunt Jenny was a devout Christian, I had no one at home to teach me how to dance, so I had to learn the hard and embarrassing way on the dance floor, while stepping on my partner's shoes. Even though I never became proficient, I enjoyed the feel of the soft female body and the aroma of feminine hair and perfume. The older girls would snatch me up from my seat and insist that I dance, and so I did, sensing my appeal to the softer sex.

My first date with a girlfriend turned out to be a disaster. I met an attractive girl, who lived on Martine Avenue in Fanwood. I can't quite recall how we met, but I became enamored with her and agreed to accompany her to a movie in Plainfield, where she apparently used to live. It was in winter or early spring because I was wearing a 3-quarter coat over the 3-piece suit I had bought.

I don't remember the movie because I was infatuated with her. When the movie ended and we walked outside of the old Paramount Theater and approached the bus stop, a group of Black guys followed us out, but they walked down the other side of the street and huddled. As our city bus neared, one of the guys called my date to come over and talk. I stayed put at the bus stop. When she returned, she said I should get on the bus first because those guys knew I was from Scotch Plains and might attack me.

When the bus arrived, I insisted that she board first but the gang charged me and began punching and kicking me up against the bus. I fought back as best I could, protecting my head as I scrambled up into the bus. The driver was frozen stiff and wouldn't close the door. Fortunately, an older black passenger came to my aid and threatened my tormentors with his pocketknife while telling the driver to pull off. This man, who I believe saved my life, got off the bus at Cottage Street, and I never saw him again.

As I sat there with my date, I realized that I had a swollen eye and scratches and cuts on my face, which she tended to as best she could. She got off the bus on Park Avenue, where her mother or father waited to pick her up, while I sat there in a state of shock and embarrassment, enduring the stares and comments until the bus stopped in Jerseyland. I don't recall ever seeing or talking with the girl after that night. I walked home in silence and went immediately down into the basement kitchen. Joe was home and came down to see what had happened. By then, my eye was all puffed up and swollen and I looked awful and felt angrier, rather than hurt.

When Daddy learned what happened to me, he was anything but sympathetic, reminding me of his warnings about going out to parties. "Where are your friends now!" he yelled. "Why didn't they help you up there?" he continued. I sulked and licked my wounds. Although I was crushed emotionally, I was not broken.

A SIGN TO CHANGE AND DIRECT MY OWN PATH

Aunt Jenny prayed for me after the attack and asked me to pray for guidance and God's protection. "It's a sign," she told me, "that I needed to change my ways." I came to this realization also and went about the change alone. I went to school, and my job, but I avoided the local hangouts. I began asking myself what I wanted to do with my life, and how I could avoid future trouble. The answer was to bury myself in schoolwork, my job and church activities.

Two weeks after those guys jumped and beat me in Plainfield, some of them were involved in a serious stabbing incident, resulting in the death of a 32-year-old man at a birthday party. This news was very sobering to me and strengthened my resolve to stay clear of parties, dances and the roller-skating rink on Park Avenue in Plainfield, where teens congregated on weekends and was often the site of fights between gangs. It was also the place where Plainfield and Roselle guys usually had altercations.

St. John's Baptist Church was our family's church, located just a block away, at the end of Park Place. Joe and I were both baptized there in the small pool under the floor, behind the pulpit. I remember being dunked in the water and holding my nose. I'm not sure of the minister's name who baptized me, but when he retired, he was replaced by a younger man, Reverend Glover, a seminary graduate and the son of a well-known minister.

Reverend Glover was married, had children and quickly gained a reputation as a powerful speaker, which increased the congregation immeasurably. He was especially interested in involving more young people in church activities, and I started attending services more regularly and participating in programs for youth. I remember reading a passage from the Bible, and once offering a short prayer.

My friend and I conducted a service once on a day, devoted to the youth of the church. He read a scripture and I delivered a short sermon, which was well-received and drew much praise. Many of the parishioners said that I sounded like real preacher, and some predicted that I would become a minister. I must say that this occasion was a confidence-builder for me. I noticed how some people looked at me differently and took more time to converse with me about serious issues.

In 1957, the church sponsored a bus trip to Madison Square Garden in Manhattan, where evangelist Billy Graham was holding a revival. Daddy and I joined the group, and we tried to sit in the same row so as not to get separated at the end of the program. However, I was so moved by Graham's sermon that I got up and walked down to the front of the auditorium with hundreds of others who answered the call to give our lives to Jesus Christ. I was so swept up in the emotion of the moment that I didn't tell Daddy what I was doing, so I got separated from the group, who had to wait for me to return to the bus.

On the bus ride home, I was the subject of conversation and felt somewhat surprised and embarrassed by what I had done. Apparently, I was the only one from our church to answer Reverend Graham's call. I'm sure that I was the youngest member of our group. Since I was already baptized and a church member, some wondered why I felt the urge to answer Graham's call. I attribute it to the power of his sermon, especially when he described perfectly how I was feeling at that moment.

Our own reverend was ambitious and determined to make St. John's his church. Despite a disagreement about demolishing the old building, he prevailed, and his new church, which was a dome with a rectangular annex, was the first of its kind in the area. It attracted many curious folk from near and far away. It got ample photo coverage in the local newspaper as well and the congregation increased as predicted.

Eventually, my father, an usher, fell out with the reverend because of the way he operated and the demands he made on the congregation. So Daddy began having Jehovah's Witness visitors come to the house and discuss the Bible, and eventually my sisters were included in these Bible lessons. Despite the issues with the reverend, he wrote a letter of reference for me as I applied for admission to Hampton, and members of the church took up a collection of over one hundred dollars to help me with my college expenses.

SHAPING OF A SCHOLAR – THE FORMATIVE YEARS

My earliest memory of being in school was enjoying my black and gray rug in kindergarten. I suppose I still remember it because I used it at home long after I graduated from the 6th grade and moved on to the middle school on Park Avenue. School #3 in Jerseyland, which was our neighborhood school for kindergarten through grade 6, where most of the students were black, except for a few white kids on Waldheim Avenue. However, all the teachers and the principal were white.

The principal, Mr. Keys, was a strict disciplinarian who had previously been a correctional officer or administrator. He had a glass eye, due to some accident in his youth, and he was especially hard on those caught throwing stones or snowballs. His favorite punishment for rule breakers was an hour walking along the fence. His usual habit was to grab a kid by the ear and walk him to his office, threatening to "wax your red wagon." One student, an orphan in particular, was his main victim. We all predicted that he would one day turn on the principal and get his revenge, but he never did. I often wonder what happened to him.

Besides my problems with the principal, I recall being one of the student safety patrols. My picture appeared in the local paper, the *Plainfield Courier News*, and Mom got several copies of the clipping from neighbors. I was also good at spelling and won the Spelling Bee contest with another student, who became Joe's first wife.

As a 7th grader, I excelled in English, History and Geography. My Geography teacher made class interesting with his war stories. We would try to get him talking about his times in World War II battles in France and Italy. I was good at remembering names, places and stories from the textbook. I would write down the specifics, and this helped me do well on tests. However, I was lost in Math class. Too embarrassed to ask her for extra help, I did poorly and hence I had to repeat the 7th grade. I don't recall my parent's reaction to this failure, but I did much better the second time around with regained confidence.

What I remember most vividly about my 8th grade experience was my English class, which was taught by Mr. Herrick, a tall, well-dressed and serious man who managed the class in a no-nonsense manner. Rather than yell at an errant student, he would tap the chalkboard with his ring and point his index finger, indicating what he wanted the kid to do. Usually, it was a direction to sit down or be quiet; but when he focused on you and pointed to the door, it meant "go to the principal's office." Sometimes when he got really irritated, he would hit the board with such force that we thought it might crack. I don't recall being a problem for him.

I was feeling very creative at this time and began writing "My Life," a biography in pencil on sheets of Math paper. My classmates became interested and asked to read some pages. One day the teacher asked if he could read it over the weekend. Of course, I was thrilled. When he returned on Monday, he handed me a bound copy of my "book," which he prepared. It was typed neatly, but he did not correct my errors and said it was a major accomplishment for an 8th grader. I was on cloud nine and the "talk" of my classmates.

My teacher was very instrumental in helping to build my self-confidence and belief in the power of the written word. My interest in creative writing received another boost in another English class, when our teacher asked us to write a letter about any topic we wished. So I wrote an essay, focused on how much I enjoyed nature and outdoor activities. When I received my essay back with detailed comments, my teacher applauded my vivid description and word usage while encouraging me to continue writing.

Of all of my classes, History was my favorite. I was one of the top students in a class taught by an energetic fellow, who seldom sat at his desk, instead moving around the classroom. He used the chalk board to emphasize the important themes and facts, and I usually wrote it all down. To those kids who he caught looking out the window or being inattentive, he said, "You won't find the answer there," or "there won't be no Santa Claus in June." He was very expressive during his lectures, sticking out his tongue and shaking his head. His class was always interesting and entertaining.

In my junior and senior years, I was interested in U.S. History. I bought and read best sellers, like *Andersonville* by McKinley Kantor, and *The Etruscans* by Barker. When we focused on the Civil War, I bought a 4-volume history, *Battles and Leaders of the Civil War*. On one hand, one of my teachers was very inspiring because of his approach to the subject and his mild and caring teaching style. He was very helpful and sympathetic, and he shared his personal experiences with us

Because I was interested in the Civil War, I wrote my term paper on the first battles at Bull Run, while for my other History teacher who besides teaching English classes, was also the varsity football coach and not one of my favorite teachers. He loved to embarrass students who talked out of turn or who weren't paying attention. He was especially tough on the girls in class. He gave me a B on my paper, and red inked my typos and spelling errors, though he complimented me on my theme and organization. At that point, I was seriously focused on going to college. Teachers and counsellors insisted that only those who wrote a term paper would be eligible for an honors grade.

There was a very dapper, smooth and erudite man who taught Economics to mainly seniors, who were all male. Only one female had enrolled, but she dropped the course, to feeling uncomfortable. Nevertheless, the teacher entertained us with anecdotes about the difficult times during the Great Depression when he was a young father. Times were really hard for people in all classes of society, and he admitted stealing milk from the truck when he couldn't afford to buy any for his baby. He kept our attention while describing how many wealthy stockholders committed suicide, jumping from tall buildings in 1929. But we also learned how to manage money, checking and savings accounts and government bonds. He told us to always save 10 percent of earnings for the rainy day, which we could always expect.

MATURITY, MANHOOD AND MOVING ON

Through my high school years, I had some confrontations with some kids, like Gene Hall, who challenged me to a fight after school during the 9th or 10th grade. After we both sustained some bruises and scrapes, we stopped and shook hands, indicating a new mutual respect.

As a junior during football season, I had to punch a teammate, who tried to push me out of the shower. I broke his nose and was afraid that there would be repercussions, because his father was a policeman with a bad reputation. The father was one of the customers on my after-school paper route, but he never spoke to me about the altercation.

That was my last fight in school, and teachers and fellow students saw me as a serious student who didn't engage in name-calling and pranks. I had lifted weights, strengthened my body and commanded some degree of respect from most of my classmates, including John Andruski, the class bully, whose father was a policeman. He used to pick on certain guys, but he never bothered with me.

I participated in track, and I also played on the football team as a linebacker on defense, and guard, on offense. I endured for 3 years but there were usually bigger guys who got the first-string positions. So I devoted my senior year to focusing on working in the afternoons and saving money for college, which was not a difficult decision because I disliked the coach.

When it came time to consider college, some of the neighbors said I should have applied to Rutgers, but I wanted to attend an out-of-state school. More correctly, I wanted to experience a different environment than that in Scotch Plains. Therefore, I applied to Hampton Institute in Hampton, Virginia, for early admission, and though I don't recall taking an SAT or any such test, both my grades and my references were good and strong enough to be accepted.

My father's sister, Esther Early, lived in Hampton, and she influenced my decision to attend. The fact that the college was near the bay was also a plus. Joe and I had driven down for a visit earlier, and I knew a local guy who was stationed at Langley Air Force Base, who spoke highly of the college. I did not attempt to get a football scholarship, because my high school record was not that impressive. However, when I arrived on campus, I decided to try out for the Hampton Pirates Football Team and was a walk-on. I played for 3 years, but I never became a letterman. I was the second-string center and played in a several games.

CHALLENGES, COEDS AND CAMPUS LIFE

As the day for leaving for Hampton approached, I was excited at the prospect of this watershed experience. I can honestly say that I really wanted to get away, not so much from family and home, but rather from the larger community. I was looking forward to living on a campus with educated people of color. Most of my neighbors who attended college had assured me I would enjoy the new environment and make new friends. So I worked right through my last day, trying to earn and save as much as I could to cover my tuition. I assumed that the yearly cost of attending Hampton, $905, could be paid by my savings, with help from my parents. We did not anticipate borrowing money, but I didn't account for other expenses.

Daddy liked to drive at night, so we took off at midnight in his 1950 Plymouth, which he had painted red. Of course, we had the obligatory packed lunch of sandwiches that Mom prepared, as Daddy was not fond of stopping at restaurants on the road. Traffic was light along the New Jersey Turnpike, through Delaware, Maryland and Virginia on U.S. Route 13. We took the Cape Charles Ferry across to Hampton Roads and arrived at Aunt

Esther's house in Hampton. She and Uncle Ferd lived on Union Street, about two miles from the campus. They were glad to see us and had a nice brunch prepared. I was not really hungry, having eaten most of the lunch on the trip, but they insisted that I eat, because it would be my last home-cooked meal for a while.

The campus was as beautiful as I remembered from my first visit. We parked in front of my dorm, which was in James Hall, and found my room, (617) on the first floor. My roommate was not there, but his jacket was draped over one of the chairs. Daddy said that he must be a big fellow, since the jacket sleeves were touching the floor. I picked up my orientation packet from the office and met a few of my fellow classmates. After Daddy left, I unpacked my luggage and sat at my desk, reviewing the various forms and course offerings.

The room was larger than the bedrooms at home. There was a single bed, a desk and a chair on each side of the room, and a closet. There was also enough room for small bookshelves (if we wanted them) and rugs. The building was a 5-story brick structure, located at one end of the campus, which was a considerable walk to the Virginia Cleveland Dining hall, where the underclass girls were housed.

Robert Raney, my roommate, returned to the room after lunch. He was indeed a big guy who was 6' 4" and was at least 230 lbs. He wore a size 15 shoe and complained about his foot problems, which allowed him an exemption from ROTC. He was from Suffolk, Virginia. He had been on campus many times and was familiar with the surrounding towns as well. He had secured a part-time job in the nearby crab factory, just across the bridge from campus.

Robert was not an athlete, but his size was somewhat of a deterrent to upperclassmen, who dropped by to give us the usual taunting dished out to freshmen. We both agreed that we would not yield to any ridiculous demands, like counting the graves in the nearby veterans' cemetery. Robert was a math major, and he liked to have the radio on while doing his homework, which I found distracting. I found that I could get more work done in the library.

That first day on campus was exhausting; getting checked in at the dorm, looking over our orientation materials, visiting the laundry building and going to the gym, located at the far end of campus. We had to get a post office box and arrange for a student bank account, which was optional. Dinner was in Virginia Hall, cafeteria style, and the food was rich, while the servings were plentiful.

Besides getting settled in, I was busy checking out the many pretty coeds, who were also looking at us. This was my first time seeing so many attractive Black girls, but I was a little shy and didn't try to get acquainted with any. Robert, on the other hand, seemed to know a few of the girls and enjoyed introducing me. It was clear that he thought himself a "ladies' man," and he delighted in saying which girls were interested in me.

After dinner, we all gathered in Ogden Hall, the main auditorium for words of welcome from the deans. When we returned to our dorms, there were more meetings and introductions for the dorm staff. Unlike the girls' dorms, James Hall was not locked at night, and there were no prohibitions on our coming and going, but it was expected that we would settle down by 10:30 p.m. Eventually, each floor developed a consensus on appropriate and inappropriate behavior.

The next day, we had registration for classes. This was simple for freshman because most of us had to take standard core courses in oral and written communication, math, U.S. History, physical education and ROTC. Since Hampton was a land grant institution, ROTC was required for two years. I enjoyed and excelled in U.S. History. Written Communication was more arduous, especially with a professor who seemed more impressed with grammar skills than good ideas.

Math proved once again to be my nemesis, since the instructor seemed to enjoy belittling students rather than commiserating. Consequently, I failed the course. Years later, several other students told me about how much they disliked his class. Physical Education was enjoyable and since I was on the football team, the coach exempted me from some ordeals. I did have to pass the required swimming test, which entailed swimming 4 pool-lengths uninterrupted. ROTC class was in the afternoon, and it involved weapons instruction, marching skills, military courtesy and obedience and military history.

My first semester academic performance was quite sobering, and in some instances, humiliating. I discovered how much more demanding the professors were and where I ranked among my classmates. Many of them were from middle-class and professional backgrounds, very bright, sophisticated, and cosmopolitan. There were foreign students from African countries or colonies, some from Asia, and a few Hungarians. Hampton was proud of its small group of white students from the surrounding towns and military bases. The campus was near Fort Monroe, Fort Eustis, Langley Air Force Base and Norfolk Naval Station, which allowed for cooperative activities with ROTC.

Photos - Section One

Baby Joe Henry Davis, III
and Linda Davis - 1935

Grandma Linda Craft-Davis with Joe Henry in
Chatham, 1936

Aunt Jenny Craft-Hardnett

Gale's grandparents, Rev. and Mrs. Ella Reid, Columbus, GA, 1940s

George Davis, sister Sally Ramsey and husband.

Photos - Section One

Mother Gertrude with Aunt Philly and friend, Robert, Westfield, NJ, 1932

Brother Joe and his buddies, me and their puppies at home

Joe and me in Chatham, 1947

Gert and Acie

Waverly Craft, brother of Linda Davis
1930s or 1940s

Isaac and Nancy Stewart, Bordentown, NJ

Photos - Section One

Dad in uniform

Mom in the yard

Part Two

TEACHINGS TO LAST A LIFETIME—FACULTY REVIEWS

The president of the college was a handsome, light-skinned man from the Virgin Islands. I never had any close contact with him, and I think he did a lot of fundraising off-campus. He did not appear to be interested in the day-to-day student/faculty life. In 1958, he retired and was replaced by dean of faculty. Like most students, I had little contact with members of the administration.

Having failed math in the first semester, I was determined to get more serious about my studies. I developed the habit of spending two and a half hours after dinner in the library, doing homework. There were study booths in the back, beyond the stacks, and it was quiet and conducive to concentration. I decided to test my resolve by walking from James Hall and past the evening softball game on Bemis lawn, where my guys and girls were playing, and head straight for the library. This study schedule was very effective, because I was able to pass Math and do very well in my other courses.

Another one of the professors who helped me develop more self-confidence taught Speech, or Oral Communication, and he required each student to deliver short speeches that he criticized severely until we perfected the skill. His final exam involved our speaking on the stage in Ogden Hall, while he sat in the balcony listening. His famous warning was, "You got to MOVE me," meaning he expected a lively and enthusiastic performance. I did well after a slow start and many corrections of diction and pronunciation. I didn't realize I was saying "git" instead of "get" or "necked" for "naked."

Mr. Bolton was very neat and dapper and almost effeminate in the way he walked, but he was cognizant that people were whispering about it. "If you think I'm gay, ask my wife," he said to the class one day. His wife was an artist, specializing in watercolor paintings, and they had two children. I got to know the family well and was hired to take his wife's mother on walks (she was on a walker) and do minor physical therapy exercises.

One of my history instructors was a typical New England Yankee who was an effective teacher, but he was not one for after class chats with students. He recognized my interest and ability and graded my work accordingly. Mr. Lewis enjoyed class discussions more than giving lectures. He had been a part of the Federal Writers Project in the 1930s, and he was determined that we should know more about African American

History than the textbook offered. He would sit on the desk, smoking a cigarette, telling us about famous Black leaders and how they impacted American History. For me like most students, these talks were real eye openers, often prompting after class discussions on the merits of African and African American History courses.

Our European History professor, Dr. Young, broadened his curriculum to include units on Africa and Asia. He was a bachelor and a real scholar who did detailed research and often shared his findings with us. He required several short essays and one longer term paper in addition to his unit test and occasional quizzes.

As a stickler for facts to support generalizations, he was not opposed to giving failing grades. When a student asked him why he gave him an "E+" on a test, the professor snorted and said, "Well, I can change it to an E-," which drew a laugh from the class. I took detailed notes in class and on the readings, and this helped me especially on the tests and quizzes. I got "A"s in all his courses. When I graduated, he gave me a camera for my forthcoming trip to Liberia.

Dr. Thomas White taught Economics, which all History and Social Science majors had to take and pass with a "C." He was very unpopular. He primarily lectured and gave multiple choice and true/false exams. He did not like to be challenged in class, and he seldom spent time after class in meaningful conversations with students. I got to know his wife and often had pleasant conversations with her. I judged from those talks that she was lonely and not happy in her marriage. Even though I feared her husband would flunk me, I made it through with a "B-."

Although we were required to take Social Philosophy for graduation, many in my class didn't like the professor. While I didn't enjoy his style of teaching, I did my best to satisfy the requirement. Some of the girls in class discovered the benefits of getting help during the professor's office hours. One attractive girl even sat on his desk during a conference, and she got an "A."

Political Science was also required for graduation. Most students took this course as sophomores, so the professor was accustomed to lecturing without interruptions. It was clear he didn't like students to question his ideas. When I took the course in my senior year and disagreed with his interpretation of Thomas Jefferson's concept of liberty and equality, I emphatically stated that I thought Jefferson was a hypocrite. The professor sternly disagreed, saying I was too harsh on the founder.

At final exam time, he was supposed to meet me at a different time, as senior exams were scheduled earlier. When he failed to appear, I had the right to not take the exam, but another professor urged me to call my professor and set a time for the exam. When we met, he handed me an exam, which I needed to pass with a "C" in order to graduate. He let me squirm for a day, however, before telling me my grade, which was a "C+." He often told us in class that the final exam was the most important grade, "because it's not how you begin the race that counts, but how you end it." I was glad to end it.

The supervisor of student teaching was a no-nonsense person. She held conferences with the seniors and our teachers. She demanded that we show her our teaching units and lesson plans, which she reviewed and criticized. She often told the senior, "If you can't explain it to me, how are you going to explain it to your students?" Our units had to be typed in triplicate, which involved two carbon sheets.

I was paired with a biology major and an English minor, and the supervisor expected me to lead during the conferences. On the first day in the course, when the professor examining our class schedules realized I didn't have mine, she quipped, "Well, what did you come for? To add dignity to the class?" I got teased about this for a long time. Nonetheless, I received an "A" from her.

George Phenix High School was one of the two Black high schools in Hampton. It was adjacent to the campus, and the building was leased to the town. This is where my practice at teaching took place. In the fall semester, I was assigned to Mrs. Cook's World History class. She was an astute, professional teacher, a stickler for the rules, and she did not leave me alone in the class. She insisted on seeing my lesson plan, which had to include everything I planned to say—even the questions for discussions. She assured me that the students would be impressed by my preparation.

In the spring, I taught U.S. History in Mrs. Neilson's class. She was much more relaxed and confident in my ability to handle the class. Sometimes she even left me alone to conduct the lesson, and fortunately I did okay.

LIFE IN JAMES HALL: NEW FRIENDS

The dorm was occupied mainly by freshman, but a few older students and veterans lived there as well. Frank Baker and Salvadore Perry lived on my wing, just two doors away. Frank, who had served in the Army, was from Martinsville, Virginia, and he was majoring in Engineering. Salvadore was a Navy vet from North Carolina whose major was Early Childhood Education. We became good friends. I can still picture Salvadore on his way to the bathroom, wrapped in his bath towel, saying, "It's time to shit, shave, and shower." He was a lively fellow and became a school principal in North Carolina. I was able to attend Frank's wedding in Martinsville, since I was in Chatham at the time.

Emmett Beckett was an older guy and veteran who lived on the top floor in a single room. Quite eccentric, he was an Art major, specializing in pottery. He had attended Hampton earlier and was a critic of the Black bourgeoise and the policies of the college administration. His room reeked of a mixture of nicotine and his body odor, as he was a chain smoker who seldom changed his sheets. Once when he took the sheets to the laundry, a lady criticized him in front of some coeds, which really angered him. He and I became friends, as I learned many details about throwing pots and making glazes from him and our art professor. Unfortunately, he did not graduate with us in 1961 and I lost touch with him.

Hampton welcomed many foreign students, like Assibi Abado from Ghana who was about 25 years old. He had been a policeman who also lived in a single on the 5th floor. He wore shorts year-round, and when I asked how he could endure the cold weather, he would say that it didn't bother him. He was a striking figure, walking at a brisk pace across the campus, always happy and cheerful. In the dining hall, his meals were specially prepared, as he was a vegetarian. Guys would ask him about eating so many boiled eggs and having gas. He would claim that he could control expelling gas, that it was "all in the mind."

Zuhair Hamdan was a Palestinian from Israel who was fluent in English, but he had a heavy accent. I had conversations with him about his religion, Islam, which I was studying in history class. In our text, the Prophet Muhammad was described as a leader who conquered territory in the name of Allah. Zuhair emphasized the teachings of the Koran, which were about "Submission" and the peaceful aims of the religion.

The guys in the dorm with whom I developed lasting friendships were Doug Jones, McCall Skeeter and my roommate. We all lived on the first floor. Doug roomed with Rudolph Morbay, a Hungarian, who escaped from his Communist controlled country in 1956. Rudy and I were on the swimming team together; he was our top backstroke swimmer and adjusted well as the only white guy on the team. We had some good times on the "away" meets in West Virginia, Baltimore, and Washington D C. Another Hungarian, Andras Kovacs, was later admitted as a freshman and roomed with Rudy, while Doug moved to Harkness Hall with Mende Terrefe, who was related to an Ethiopian icon.

Terrefe was an older guy, partially bald, with soft, curly, dark hair and a light tan complexion. He was about 5'6" and had a pleasant, engaging personality. He smoked one cigarette after another and found it difficult to attend Chapel or other all school events where smoking was not allowed. He was a natural with women and had girlfriends off campus. Although Terrefe did not share many details of his background, he was nervous about the events taking place in Ethiopia, where Haile Selassie had been overthrown in a *coup d'etat*. I think he was sympathetic with the young revolutionaries and worried about his own safety if the *coup* was not successful. I lost touch with him after graduation.

BECOMING A HAMPTON PIRATE:
FOOTBALL AND SWIMMING

I did not initially plan to try out for the football team, but after watching the team practice, and realizing that I could contribute, I decided to join. It was not difficult. The coach sent me the equipment room, where other coaches fitted me with a practice uniform and pads and told me to go out there and *Show us what you can do.* So I gave my best effort to the wind sprints, calisthenics and laps around the field. Pushing the sled, blocking the pad held by a coach and live one-on-one blocking proved challenging, but I performed well. The real test came when the coach put me in a scrimmage as a defensive guard, facing our junior tackle, Adrian Nelson, whose elbow collided with my nose and upper lip.

I continued to play with blood trickling down, until the coach called me to the bench to be treated by the manager. I guess that was my test, which I passed, because I overheard some of the older players saying I was "tough." They soon gave me the nickname "Red," which I was already accustomed to from my days as a caddy. When the coach posted the list of team members and their positions, my name was there as a guard. It was comforting to have a "sense of belonging" on the team.

Since I had played as a guard in high school, I continued in that position on offense and played linebacker on defense. I was quite fast—not as quick as the running backs, but I could catch and tackle backs on end-runs. When the coach saw how determined I was to mix it up and hit hard, I got more opportunities to play. However, there always seemed to be a bigger and taller guy playing the same position who was put in the games, while I sat on the bench.

When the second-string center position opened, I tried out for it and won. I remember practicing punt passing, which a center must do, and I learned the various plays. I weighed about 195 pounds as a sophomore, and while I lifted weights and did bodybuilding exercises, I was still small as a center. I found this out during the first game. I got to play for a few minutes when Frank Smith, the varsity center, was resting, or when he was injured.

During the game at Morgan State University in Baltimore, I played most of the second half, while Frank sat injured on the bench. The big middle guard who stood over me kept trash-talking me, and after I snapped the ball, he pushed me into the backfield. I will never forget that game, played in the rain and mud, and the humiliating loss to a bigger and faster team. During the trip back to Hampton, our bus broke down in a town called "Ordinary," Virginia.

During my junior year, my third season on the team, I had become frustrated with sitting on the bench. Frank would often gesture for me to "just get off the bench" and run in, but I would not do that without the coach's okay. During home games, I recall seeing Salvadore Perry, sitting in the bleachers, yelling, "put # 55 in!" which was my number, but Coach Whaley would not comply. The away game at Johnson C. Smith University in Charlotte, N.C., involved a long bus ride and overnight stay. During the game, Sal was limping, but Coach Whaley would not put me in the game, despite Sal's efforts to get me in.

Upon returning to Hampton, I found the door to my room open and my money and Avon order missing. This proved to be enough reason to quit the team, since I realized that Coach Whaley did not intend to give me significant playing time. When I spoke to Whaley before Monday practice, he insisted that he would know when I was ready, but I told him I was quitting the team.

He tried to cancel my grant-in-aid of $250, but I continued to receive this benefit for the rest of the year. I was hurt by not receiving "a Letter" after practically 3 years, after having never missed a practice. I thought of Dad's comment about coaches taking players for granted.

I joined the swimming team, as Coach Moore believed I could contribute at the 50-yard freestyle and butterfly events. I had been swimming since I was a kid back home, but this competitive professional swimming was a real challenge. We practiced at 6 a.m. and 4 p.m. My effort to become a butterfly competitor was disappointing. I had my moment of glory during our meet at home against West Virginia State, when I won the freestyle relay to seal our victory. Rudy won the backstroke and the breaststroke events. I earned a letter as a swimmer, but I was not a member of the Varsity club.

At Morgan State, I competed in the 440 and the mile events, but I was only swimming as an extra and not expected to win. My left leg gave out after 21 laps. During our away meet at Howard University, the small pool was more of a problem than the competition. We spent the night at Stowe Hall. Someone kept starting fires in the dorm, so we had to go out into the courtyard to escape the smoke. It was February and cold, which made it a real drag. The culprit was not found while we were there. I don't recall which team won the meet, but we were under pressure to win, as Howard was our big rival. Howard was the most prestigious of the historically Black colleges.

The Hampton men had an initiation practice, called "greasing," which involved seizing a guy, usually in the shower or the locker room when he was undressed. His tormenters then sprayed or squirted or smeared some Vaseline, toothpaste or something similar on his buttocks. The victim was expected to put up a struggle, so it took 3 or 4 guys to successfully accomplish the act.

If the guy didn't fight hard or at all, he was thought to be gay. (Note: There were a number of gays at Hampton—some openly effeminate and others closet cases. During that era, gays and lesbians were ridiculed, especially those who came out of the closet, but most Hamptonians were very tolerant.)

The initiations usually took place on away games and were inflicted by senior or upper classmen on freshmen. It got very rough sometimes, and some guys got bruised or cut or scratched up a bit. Occasionally, a fight would breakout between the victim and one of his tormentors. Some big or well-built guys would avoid the initiation until their senior year or completely altogether.

I never participated in a "greasing" incident, because I thought it was primitive and disgusting; but I also hoped my attitude might prevent me being a victim. However, as a junior on the swimming team (even though I was pumped up from weightlifting), there were guys who tried to get me anyway. After our competition at Morgan State, a few of my teammates tried to initiate me, but I put up such a struggle that they couldn't get me down, so they smeared some toothpaste on my neck and back and quit.

GIRLS AND GIRLFRIENDS

One of my earliest observations upon arriving on campus was the number of pretty girls and female faculty and staff. Walking from James Hall to the dining hall or the canteen, I noticed some girls watching me as much as I was watching them. There were a couple of upper-class girls from New Jersey who called me "Homeboy" and talked to me in the canteen. One of them had a scarf with the map of New Jersey on it, and she tried to find Scotch Plains, but she couldn't. That was the cue for Everett Brawner, a freshman from Georgia, to pull down his pants and suggest we look for my hometown on his ass. That got a big laugh.

The dining hall was the natural meeting place for couples. Like most guys, I sat with fellows I knew, usually from the dorm, or the football team. After dinner, we lingered outside on the steps, we talked with girls and walked with them down to the waterfront, to the Canteen or back to their dorms. As a member of the football team, I enjoyed a slightly higher profile during meals, because athletes were entitled to extra beverages and other treats.

During lunch, we filed in together, and relished the attention from girls. One freshman co-ed named Emogene Newby from Norfolk approached me and asked why I always sit with the guys. We talked after dinner and walked for a while before I escorted her to her dorm. She was the aggressor in our brief relationship, which involved walks along the bay, holding hands and kissing. I don't recall exactly why we stopped hanging out together, but I think we had conflicting expectations of each other.

There were a few other girls that I pursued and enjoyed spending time with, either in the library while studying or walking into town to shop or escorting them to a campus movie or dance. Under the cover of darkness, we engaged in the typical necking and fondling as much as the girl allowed. The deans made it clear that students were expected to honor the rules about sexual intercourse. Campus security would occasionally discover a couple having sex and report it. Some couples went to local motels to consummate their relationships. I will only say here that I respected the girls wishes during these affairs.

I did have a serious relationship with a classmate named Gertrude. Her father had been a member of the faculty, and she was familiar with the campus and the other faculty and staff families. Her home was in another Virginia town, but she lived on campus when we were together. She was an English major, an Honors student and exchange student in the spring semester of our junior year at Madison College.

We really enjoyed being together, sharing many ideas and opinions, and corresponding regularly during the summer. I had dinner at her home and got to know her parents and brothers well. Like Gertrude, they were very light-skinned, with fine smooth hair.

Even though Gertrude could easily pass for white, she told me about incidents where she had to make it clear that she was not white. Once when the two of us were waiting for the bus just off campus, some Black guys driving by yelled to me, "Man you better watch what you doing!" Gertrude asked me what that was all about, but I think she knew. We talked about it during the ride to her home. After she returned from Madison, we drifted apart. We remained friends and kept in touch for the next 5 years. She married a professor at Wesleyan State University, and they had a little boy. By then it was 1966, and I had gotten married and was living in Massachusetts.

LIVING WITH JIM CROW

Although I was raised in New Jersey and did not experience *"de jure"* racial segregation, I was certainly aware of the racism below the Mason-Dixon line. During the several trips "down south" with my brother and father, we didn't encounter any overt racism.

My brother, Joe, was stopped for speeding once in Fairfax, Virginia, and the State Trooper was a little acerbic, but there was no hint of racism during the traffic stop and the appearance before the judge. Daddy was quite anxious, however, and talked about being careful driving in Virginia. Joe got a ticket for speeding in Seaford, Delaware, while driving me to Hampton, but the trooper was fair and courteous.

In the 1950s, several racial incidents captured the attention of people throughout the country. This was the beginning of the Negro Revolution in the South, and Black citizens were challenging the rules blocking their voting rights, access to public accommodations and equal treatment during bus and train travel. As a serious history student in high school, I was aware of the murder of Emmett Till in Mississippi, and I had seen the unabridged photo of his body in *Jet* magazine, in which had been beaten and disfigured beyond recognition. I was also aware of the Montgomery Bus Boycott and Rosa Parks' courageous stand against segregated buses. However, my travel into the land of Jim Crow had been in cars, and we usually didn't stop at restaurants because we carried our own lunch.

My first experience of being refused service in a restaurant was on the Cape Charles Ferry in Virginia. Joe drove me down to school in his new Ford sedan. We followed Route 13 from Delaware down to Cape Charles. We had to wait an hour for the arrival of the ferry, and after we boarded, we went upstairs to the eatery to order a sandwich. We were aware that there was a separate "Colored" dining room, but Joe insisted on being served in the "White" section.

The waitress told us, "Y'all have to go to the "colored section," but we insisted on being served where we were sitting. When she realized that we weren't leaving, she just took our order anyway and we got served. I think we actually took our food and returned to the car. When we told Uncle Ferd about it, he said that "it happens sometimes, which shows how silly the whole system is." Some of the white clerks and waitresses didn't agree with denying blacks service, but if their supervisor was a real racist and threatened to fire them, they followed the rule.

Living on the Hampton campus protected us from most of the indignities that blacks experienced in the surrounding communities; but when we ventured into town for a movie, dinner or even medical care, we faced segregated facilities. If you went to a white doctor, he usually had a separate waiting room for "coloreds".

There was also a Black hospital in Hampton, where some students received care. Most of us were cared for by the college physician in the infirmary. There were two local Black dentists also available for students. On the local buses, while Blacks could sit anywhere, many sat in the rear.

There was a movie theater on King Street, just a short walk from campus in downtown Hampton. Blacks were required to sit in the balcony because it contained fewer seats. I don't recall ever watching a movie there. The Woolworth's and the drug store lunch counters only served whites; Blacks could order take out. The big department stores in Newport News, like Sears, also denied Black seating. Like most of my fellow students, I avoided these segregated facilities.

After the successful Montgomery Bus Boycott, Black college students began to challenge the racially segregated facilities in the surrounding towns. Hampton students answered the call to stand up and be counted, just like their brothers and sisters at North Carolina A&T College in Greensboro.

In the fall and winter months of the 1959-60 school year, Hampton students conducted organized and peaceful marches with signs off-campus, across the bridge into town. Some tried to sit at segregated lunch counters and were arrested, but there were no real ugly incidents or violence. I participated in one of those marches, but I was not interested in getting arrested. My father had warned me that he could not afford to be bailing me out of jail.

I remember participating in the protest march in downtown Newport News. I drove a group of students to the Sears parking lot and waited for them to finish the march down Jefferson Avenue and return to the lot for the ride back. We didn't want any students to wait for a ride by themselves because there were white youths who stood in the alley, taunting marchers with racial epithets and foul gestures. They would also spit at or on marchers who were disciplined and refused to react. I found this difficult to accept.

Sears department store was a special target, because it was a national chain that only upheld Jim Crow in their southern stores. One black lady from up North visiting her parents in the South was furious when denied lunch counter service at the store where she had just purchased a brand-new washer/dryer. She confronted the manager and canceled the order.

Many coeds ignored our boycott of the stores in Hampton, so we stationed guys on the bridge over Hampton Creek to block them from going into town. Of course, some went by car instead and others complained to the college administration and campus police.

Our Committee on Human Dignity met with the Mayor of Hampton, who accused protestors of being influenced by Communists and other outside agitators. We replied that we did not need Communists to tell us that we were being discriminated against and denied out constitutional rights. The racial tension was high, and a group of students got arrested, but some outside organization paid their bail.

One day, when I was driving a couple to the dentist in Phoebus, we stopped to get directions from an elderly white man, who angrily snapped, "You niggers think you so smart, find your *own* way!" and walked away. When we returned for the fall 1960 semester, the town had agreed to desegregate the movie theater and some other facilities. The public schools had begun to desegregate, but the predominately Black schools like Phenix remained open.

I kept a car on campus during my junior and senior years. I tried to avoid confrontations with the police while driving off campus, and I generally succeeded. However, on a trip to North Carolina with a few friends, a town policeman stopped me in Winton, North Carolina.

On the return ride back from a daytrip to Doug Jones' home, he, I, and two other students in the back seat were pulled over by a white cop, who shined his big flashlight on me and my passengers and asked, "Where you going?"

Apparently, the cop stopped me because I had New Jersey license plates, but he thought that the light-skinned girl in the back was white. Initially, I was getting irritated, but Doug nudged me to "cool it" and explained to the cop who the girl was. After he had made it clear that the girl was a Hampton student, the cop seemed to lose interest and let us go, saying, "Go on, and drive carefully."

BOURGEOISIE, NOT FOR ME
OPPOSITION TO EXCLUSION

Hampton Institute, like other colleges and universities, had several fraternities, sororities, and Greek-letter social clubs on campus. The Alpha Phi Alpha, the Omega PSI Phi, the Kappa Alpha PSI, were the major fraternities. The sororities included the Alpha Kappa Alpha, and the Delta Sigma Theta. There were other organizations, like Calliope Literary Society, the Ivy Leaf Club, the Pyramid Club of D.S.T., the Omicron Social Club and the Olympic Social Club. To join most of these groups, one had to have a C+ grade average, which led to their reputation as elitist and exclusive. I concluded that they were divisive.

Some of the guys and girls I became friendly with as freshmen became distant once they joined a Greek-letter club. The secrets and the experiences they endured as neophytes set them apart from non-members. They often claimed their own exclusive tables in the dining hall, where others were not welcome. Once, I was having a meeting with my student teaching partner, an AKA, in the Virginia Hall Dining room, when some of her Alpha "brothers" approached us and told me that the table was for frat members only. I was insulted and angered and replied, "I can sit anywhere I choose."

These fraternities, sororities and clubs held social greeting parties with refreshments, designed to attract new members. I attended one for the Alphas, but I never really planned to join. I had heard about the ordeals the pledges went through, and I saw examples, such as pledges wearing diapers and a crown of holly tree leaves in public. I couldn't see the value in such initiations at that time because I was not much of a "joiner." Coming from a working-class background and being the first in my extended family to attend college, I knew little about such organizations and would feel uncomfortable in such clubs.

The guys I hung out with shared my view, yet perhaps for different reasons. We considered the frat boys party animals and a reflection of bourgeoisie vanity. I'm sure that I unfairly judged most of them, but that's how I felt at the time. I began to immerse myself in revolutionary thoughts and ideas drawn from books dealing with the struggle against colonialism and Western racism. The Gold Coast Colony had won its independence from Great Britain under the leadership of Kwame Nkrumah, who had attended Lincoln University, a historically Black college in Oxford, Pennsylvania. We competed against them in football, and I remember "lions" telling me that Nkrumah was a student there.

CALL FOR SOLIDARITY
TO SURPRISE SENIOR CLASS PRESIDENCY

The spring semester of my junior year was a time of defining moments in my college experience. I quit the football team toward the end of the season because I wasn't getting enough playing time, but I was also beginning to think seriously about graduate school and a teaching position after graduation. I was doing very well in my History and English courses and considered applying to a law school, but I also realized the need to begin earning a living.

I was also interested in teaching or working abroad, especially in Africa. I really wanted to go to Ghana, which had just become independent and needed teachers and technicians from developed countries. I had talked with Assibi about Accra and other cities. In addition, Dr. Nancy

McGhee, who spent time there with her husband, had said great things about the people.

The campus hosted a conference on African and Third World Affairs, with the keynote speaker from the USAID. I was given the honor of introducing him to the student and faculty audience. I remember citing his many accomplishments and published works, and when he followed me to the podium, he pointed out how ironic it was that in his home, Tuskegee, Alabama, he had been declared illiterate because he couldn't interpret a passage of the U.S. Constitution to the satisfaction of the registrar.

He described the various tactics used to disqualify Blacks who were trying to register or vote. I was highly interested in his remarks about the educational needs of the Liberian people. At that time, I had no idea that I would become a teacher in Liberia, but my interest in working abroad was piqued.

"Male and Co-ed Relations" was the topic of evening dorm discussions, because of some incidents with girls involved in off campus trysts with soldiers on local military bases. Some girls were quoted saying that "Guys at Hampton were so lame or inexperienced, and hence not good dates." I don't quite remember what motivated me to attend the meeting in Kennedy Hall. Perhaps I felt they were talking about guys like me, but I went anyway.

After some introductory remarks, I stood and gave my frank opinion, accusing some coeds of not appreciating the gentlemen on campus, who tried to treat them like ladies, instead of one-night stands in an off-campus motel or the back seat of a car. I went further by criticizing fraternities and sororities for their big brother and little sister affairs. I accused the Greek-letter organizations of being divisive at a time when we needed campus solidarity in our struggle against racism and segregation. When the meeting was over, I was sure I had damaged my reputation with coeds, but instead, I they encouraged me to run for Senior Class President. I was obviously competing with fraternity guys, but to my surprise, I won.

Looking back on that time, I don't recall some of the leadership actions I took, but one stands out clearly. In the 1960 Presidential election, John F. Kennedy, who was supported by most students, won the election. Like many citizens, I was moved and inspired by his inaugural speech. He challenged us to, "Ask not what your country can do for you, but what you can do for your country." In my speech to my fellow seniors, I borrowed his words. At the moment, I was thinking seriously about teaching in Africa, and I was beginning the process of applying to domestic school systems and foreign service organizations.

THE EXHILIRATION OF ACHIEVEMENT
TO A LIFE-CHANGING EXPERIENCE

One weekend, a few close friends met in Doug's room on first Harkness Hall and filled out several applications for teaching and other positions. Doug was in advanced ROTC and would graduate as a commissioned Second Lieutenant in the U.S. Army. I applied for a position in a few school districts, as well as international teaching organizations. I also applied for admission to the law school at Wayne State University in Detroit. Our thought was to cast a broad net, rather than focus on one school or position, with the hope of getting accepted or hired by at least one institution.

My first response was a favorable one from Norcum High School in Portsmouth, Virginia, which was an offer to teach U.S. History at the 11th grade level. I remember the superintendent, who asked why I wanted to teach in Virginia during the interview—considering my home was in New Jersey. He was obviously concerned that I might be a radical who wanted to stir up trouble. So I told him what I thought he wanted to hear by replying that I had relatives nearby I said I liked the Tidewater area and looked forward to beginning my career there.

The following week, I got the contract, but I held onto it until I heard back from others, which came when the International Voluntary Services was looking for teachers for its program in Ghana and Liberia. I had applied for a position, and they offered me a job with their program in Liberia as a teacher/principal/technician in a rural village, because their project in Ghana was being phased out.

Eventually, Wayne State University responded, but I had made up my mind to go to Liberia. I remember the anxiety I felt as I sent the unsigned contract back to the Portsmouth School District superintendent. I was sure that accepting the International Voluntary Service's offer to teach in Liberia was what I really wanted to do. It was my chance to go to Africa, the *Homeland*, and I embraced the opportunity with pride and gusto.

My decision to go to Liberia did not sit well with some Hamptonians and people back home in New Jersey. I recall one of the deans questioning my decision, wondering why I would choose that prospect over a teaching job in the states. Some guys joked about me ending up in a big pot of stew in the jungle. I was amazed at how ignorant so many people were about Africa and its people. I was more concerned about the salary, which was not great. In fact, it was quite minimal, like the name of the organization, "International Voluntary Services." However, the opportunity for a life-changing experience dwarfed all other concerns.

My family was proud and excited at the prospect of me going abroad. The local newspaper, *THE PLAINFIELD COURIER NEWS*, featured a nice story about me and my new job, including a photo of me. I found out later that USAID did a check-up on my background, including questioning my hometown police department. Because I would be working under a state department contract, this was normal procedure. I spoke with a few of my high school classmates who heard about my upcoming travels and wished me well.

Although I was anxious to graduate, I admitted a little sadness as I prepared for the departure from my "Home by The Sea." My brother, Joe, brought Mom and my younger sisters, Lorraine and Joann, down and they stayed with Aunt Esther in town. I really don't remember the specifics of the ceremony except for the stroll around the Ogden Hall Circle and the picture-taking. My mother met some of the faculty, fellow graduates and their family members. The ordeal of cleaning out my room and packing for the ride home was one big blur. Saying goodbye to classmates, with the realization that I would not see most of them again or for years, was a little sad, but the exhilaration of our achievement was greater. ·

I had accumulated quite a collection of clay pots during my time in Art Pottery class, and afterward, my professor and Emmett teased me about trying to save every pot I threw on the wheel. A true potter was supposed to keep only the best pieces, but I wanted to have several smaller pots and ashtrays to give to friends and relatives.

My Studebaker was overloaded when I drove to Aunt Esther's house. I soon realized that I would have to replace a spring that snapped in the back on the driver's side. Fortunately, my Aunt Esther's neighbor, Mr. Bland, came to my rescue. He took me to a local junkyard, and we got the part we needed and did the repair in his backyard. He was one of the people who volunteered help when I was in need.

My trip back home was smooth, though I was a little apprehensive about being overloaded. When I got to Bordentown, New Jersey, I stopped for an overnight visit with Cousin Nancy, her husband and son. They were glad to see me, and we enjoyed a nice meal and an evening together. They kept a neat house, because Nancy was a stickler for cleanliness and order. Her yard was well kept as were the vegetable and flower gardens.

She still drove her 1953 Chevy, which was in great condition because neither her husband nor son drove. She was a devout, committed Christian and devoted time and resources to her church and community. Although she was always friendly and pleasant, she didn't suffer fools too gladly. She had great dignity and an aura of parental seriousness and responsibility. It would be two years before I would see her again after my return from Liberia.

Me and classmate in Harkness Hall, Hampton U, 1961

Me and the cast of *Antigone*
after a performance, Hampton U, 1960

Part Three

LEAVING FOR LIBERIA!

It was good to be back home with family, neighbors and friends. Everyone was congratulating me for graduating from college and especially for my upcoming trip abroad. I only had a few weeks before leaving for the International Voluntary Services (IVS) headquarters in Washington, D.C., so I couldn't get a job. I got the several inoculations required for work in Africa at Fort Monroe before leaving Hampton, but I had to get my passport, some photos and my airline tickets for the trip.

I spent time visiting people who had been especially supportive of me during my high school and college years because doing so was important to me. Some had helped me secure employment or contributed money to a church fund for my support or had simply encouraged me to "become somebody." Some of my high school classmates had married and become parents, others were in the military, and some had relocated, but I tried to talk to as many friends as I could before I left.

I took the bus to Washington and stayed with my Aunt Sally Ramsey and family before leaving for New York's Idlewild Airport. During this brief stay, I spent the day at the IVS office on Connecticut Avenue meeting the 3 other teachers on our Liberia team and going through the orientation sessions. Roger Wilder, the tall bespectacled Vermonter, was the most interesting character of the group. Harmer Weichel was perhaps the oldest, and most friendly, and Phil Jordan, a former marine, was a little reserved. We learned about the IVS team already working in Liberia under the leadership of Ron Kessler. They had been there 6 months, teaching in up-country district villages like Zorzor and Ganta, over 100 miles from the capital, Monrovia.

What I remember about my brief time there was the critical discussions about civil rights and the emergence of Minister Malcolm X that we had with one family. There was a program hosted by Mike Wallace of CBS News, which had a round-table discussion with Dr. Martin L. King, Jr., Roy Wilkins, Whitney Young, James Baldwin, and Malcolm X.

They were responding to Wallace's question about how best to move forward with desegregation in education, employment, and housing. When Malcolm spoke, he addressed mainly his fellow black leaders, telling them that it was folly to keep trying to join up with the white majority that refuses to treat them as equals.

Malcolm pointed to Wallace with that baleful stare, saying, "He may be sitting here with us now, but he doesn't want you moving into his neighborhood or sending your kids to his children's school." Then he asked, "What more do the whites need to do to show us that they don't want to integrate?"

That was the first time I had ever heard a Black man speak so frankly and honestly to whites on national television. It certainly gave me a lot to think about on the eve of my trip to Liberia as an African American teacher, going to a Black African nation to teach.

We flew from Washington's National Airport to LaGuardia. Then we took a bus to Idlewild, later renamed John F. Kennedy International Airport (JFK). I don't remember much about this transit, except that it was raining, and I noticed a big crack in the one of the terminal's cement walls. We boarded a big Pan Am 747 and took off at 9 pm.

Our first stop was in the Azores, for about 40 minutes, where we only had time for a bathroom break, and then we were off to Lisbon. There we stopped for an hour, long enough for passengers to board or deplane. It was about 6 a.m. and I was sleepy and not sure whether I went into the terminal or stayed on the plane. The next two stops were Rabat, Morocco and Dakar, Senegal.

We finally arrived in Liberia, landing at Robert's Field Airport, about 40 minutes outside of the Capital, Monrovia. It was about 3 p.m. and I remember how hot and humid it was. Upon deplaning, *Dr. Reasoner, a USAID administrator, drove us from the airport in his own car. I recall the rows of rubber trees along the road to Monrovia, as well as Liberians walking with tools and women carrying pots of various sizes on their heads.

They all seemed happy, waving at us as we passed in our air-conditioned car. I was impressed by the many banana trees, bending from the weight of the fruit. Pineapples grew in yards without grass, and most houses were mud huts with palm thatch roofs. That was our first real glimpse of indigenous African people and a degree of culture shock was setting in.

After Dr. Reasoner dropped us off at the St. Georges Hotel, I was still a little queasy from the long flight and declined the invitation to the party at USAID headquarters. Administrators warned us not to drink tap water, so I had a beer and relaxed in my room for the evening. I was surprised to learn that the hotel was practically next door to the Executive Mansion, where the Liberian president resided. It was only a 3-story building, with well-landscaped grounds, behind gates and fences. Across the street from the hotel were typical upscale shops and agencies. There was a power outage on our first night, and the generators came on to keep the air conditioning going.

The next morning, we went to USAID for our first orientation, where Dr. Reasoner introduced us to the IVS Chief of Party, Ron Kessler, as well as the director who led all up-country educational functions, and his Liberian counterpart. What I remember most vividly about that meeting was a comment Dr. Reasoner made to the 4 of us in his office. Looking and seemingly speaking to me, he told us how the Prairie View University team at the Booker T. Washington vocational school in Kakata had been a failure. He stated how they had not fulfilled their obligations and stressed that they were Black Americans who should have done better.

The encounter with Dr. Reasoner was shocking, as was his tone, so I asked why he was looking at me, as if I had a part in it. That was the first instance of American racism in Liberia I experienced; but it would not be the last. There were a few African American USAID staffers, and I later had opportunities to talk with them about the exportation of American racism. They conveyed incidents of white staff members who referred to Liberians as "monkeys" and "children," "not ready for the modern age."

MEETING THE INDIGENOUS PEOPLE UP-COUNTRY

Mammadi, the Liberian USAID mail truck driver, collected us from the hotel the next morning, and he drove us up-country to Zorzor District in the Western province, about 150 miles from Monrovia. We stopped for lunch at Stewart's Restaurant in the town of Gbandela. The Stewarts, Americo-Liberians, had immigrated as part of the Marcus Garvey "Back to Africa" movement. Mr. Stewart was the leader of the movement, and he owned a poultry farm not far from the village.

He was a heavy-set man in his late fifties, rather aloof and reserved, and he drove a Volkswagen Karmen Gia. His wife, Ma Stewart, was just the opposite; very warm and friendly. She ran the restaurant. Their son, Jimmy, about 30, was married to a village woman and was fluent in Kpelle, the local dialect. Mary Denison was Mr. Stewart's secretary/assistant, and she helped at the restaurant. I would become much better acquainted with that family after I moved from Zorzor.

The Macadam Highway ended in the town of Totota, about 90 miles north of the capital. From there, the road was red clay laterite, about 50 feet wide. During the rainy season, soft, bumpy stretches caused problems, where the roads were impassable. In the dry season, there was the ever-present dust. All along the way, we passed people who were walking and riding bicycles while usually waving and greeting us.

Mammadi stopped briefly so we could take some photos of a family, clustered around a big pan of "country chop," which is what we would be eating in Zorzor. It's a dish that consists of locally-grown rice and a sauce made with cassava or sweet potato leaves cooked with palm oil, and chicken, with Liberian peppers. It was usually too hot for our palates.

In our travels, I noticed that the houses varied in size, but most were round and constructed of mud and sticks, with palm-thatched roofs. Others were rectangular, with corrugated zinc roofs and stucco walls. Occasionally, we passed a store or café with a car or truck parked nearby, and with a few people sitting at a small table in the shade.

Most of the cars we saw were small, compact vehicles, such as Opels, and European models, with an occasional American 4-door sedan. The typical taxis were small buses or trucks, called Mammy wagons. They were painted in loud colors and had interesting signs or placards above the windshield.

The drivers were usually colorful characters who yelled, "Come now! Monrovia City! Let's go!" They packed their passengers into every seat and corner, including chickens and goats. They drove too fast and often had accidents. If they had a flat tire, all the passengers had to get out and help with the repair. There was no public transportation up-country or in the cities. People had to walk or take a taxi if they didn't own or have access to a car.

GETTING ADJUSTED IN ZORZOR

The USAID compound in Zorzor consisted of a small office building, a utility shack and a 3-bedroom, 12' x 65' mobile home, located outside the village. It was late afternoon when we arrived, and Harold Frier, IVS Assistant Chief of Party, and John Hughes were there to greet us. They were both much older—in their thirties, and they had been part of the first group of teachers to arrive.

IVS assigned John to the village of Sukrumo, which we passed on the way. Harold's village was Piye, a two-hour walk through the bush. Their houses were still under construction near their village schools, so they were staying at the compound temporarily. Roger and Harmer lodged with John in the house/office, and Phil and I stayed with John in the trailer.

After Mammadi delivered us and the mail, John, as promised, arranged a real Liberian dinner of country chop, with *fewer* peppers. Liberian peppers are small, about 2 inches long, but they are very hot. We had chicken with rice and cassava, cooked with palm oil; it was greasy, filling, and tasty. For dessert, there was pineapple upside-down cake from Ma Stewart's and sliced paupau. Our water came from a well on the compound, but it was boiled, filtered and cooled in the refrigerator. Our hosts again warned not to drink any water that had not been boiled. Harold had some bottled beer from the new Liberian Brewery in Monrovia and coke. There was no television, but we listened to the Liberian radio station as well as *Voice of America.*

As IVS rookies, our time in Zorzor was a continuation of orientation and learning the ways and customs of the indigenous rural people. In the Western Province, there were several tribal groups. The largest grouping, the Kru, lived in Zorzor and the surrounding communities. However, following the National Unification policy implemented by the president, indigenous people began more intertribal mingling and marrying.

In Zorzor, the Loma tribe was dominant, and it was the home of the Paramount Chief who controlled the surrounding villages. The local tribal people were still wedded to their traditional customs, beliefs and suspicious about foreigners attempting to introduce "changes." They were reluctant to send their girls to the new government schools until we made it a requirement for building a new village school.

I spent about one month in Zorzor before being assigned to my own village. What I remember about my time with Roger, Harmer, and Phil, was the hikes we took—first to John's village, to Piye and to the border with Sierra Leone. Piye was a long walk through the bush, and I don't recall meeting any people along the way. The village was isolated, but there was a jeep trail connecting it with the main road below Sukrumo.

All the houses were mud huts with thatched roofs; I don't remember seeing any zinc-roof houses other than John's small IVS house. The school was a traditional palm-thatched structure, open on two sides. Harold built his own house with cement blocks, made on-site with a block-making machine. The village provided some help with laborers and USAID gave the materials. Roger was so thirsty when we arrived that he took a drink from a bottle of what he thought was cold water, but it was actually white vinegar. His reaction was hilarious.

We took another walk to the Mano River, about 7 miles north of Zorzor. The river is the border with Sierra Leone. The customs official was away from his station, and after we walked across the bridge, we noticed him taking a bath in the river below. He waved and gave us the traditional greeting, but we walked back to the Liberian side without talking to him. There were no buildings other than the small custom office and a flimsy gate. Members of the Mano Tribe lived on both sides of the border and crossed it daily.

Before I relocated, we got German Zundapp motor bikes that ran on gasoline and could reach up to 80 kilometers per hour. Having our own means of transportation offered great opportunities to explore the area, which had roads and paths that were rough. Initially, we didn't have any type of Liberian documentation, so occasionally soldiers would stop us and ask for our licenses.

Ironically, the man appointed Commissioner of Public Safety tried to harass some IVS teachers as he passed in his car. He had a driver and sat in the back seat, often with a bottle in his hand. Fortunately, I never had a run-in with him. Soldiers at gates to the district towns expected a "dash," or a bribe, from foreigners before they raised the gate. They would expect a few cigarettes, coins or fruit. If we threatened to complain to the D.C., they would let us through without paying. That was the common type of corruption in most towns with public officials or soldiers. It was easier to flip them a few coins rather than incur their wrath.

"GOOD MORNING, TEACHER DAVIS!"
MY FIRST VILLAGE SCHOOL

IVS assigned me to the town of Gbartala, Central Province, on the main road, about 4 miles north of Stewart's Restaurant. It was a large town with a gas station, café and other small shops. The highway divided the town, and cars and trucks moved through, regularly leaving a dust trail and the sounding of horns. The Mammy wagon taxis stopped at the café to drop off and pick up passengers just across the road from my house. I moved in to what had been the town nurse's house, a zinc-roofed 4-room square structure of mud and sticks, with a cement stucco outer coating. It also had a covered screened porch where patients could wait to be treated. It was clearly one of the nicer buildings in town.

USAID installed my kitchen appliances, fueled by kerosene, including a refrigerator and stove. They also supplied a water filter, pots and pans, dishes and dinnerware. The other rooms were modestly furnished, with beds and chairs and a chest of drawers. The outside toilet, water closet or "WC," was being constructed in the backyard when I arrived. When I joined the laborers in digging the hole, they laughed and guffawed to see me slinging a pick. Apparently, *Kwe Quelli*—their name for whites or foreigners, were not expected to do physical labor. I made it clear that I was not white and that I was used to hard work. I soon became the talk of the town.

The major ethnic group in that area was the Kpelle tribe, one of the largest groups in the country. Gbartala was the seat of the Paramount Chief and hence the site of numerous court cases. The courthouse was in front of my dwelling, facing the road. The school building and compound were up on the hill behind Reeves' Café, across the road from my house; I had a short walk to the school.

The school building was constructed of mud and sticks, with a tarpaper roof that leaked on rainy days. It was large enough to accommodate 35 students, but on some days, 70 children were jammed into all spaces. The teacher/principal, *Mr. Adjo Kwabala, dressed neatly in Fanti-cloth shirt and slacks, managed the pupils while carrying a small stick or pointer to get their attention. There were benches for the pupils, but not enough tables or desks. The teacher's crude desk and chair were made by a local craftsman.

After moving into my house, I walked up to the school with the IVS Chief, Ron Kessler. The children gave me a big welcome, and the principal, despite being happy to see me, was anxious about whether I would be taking over the upper grades, 4th, 5th and 6th, where the students ranged from ten to twenty years of age. A couple of the older boys were already fathers, as I later discovered. They had been helping the teacher with the smaller pupils and keeping the building and grounds clean.

It was very delightful to be greeted with, "Good Morning, Teacher Davis," at the beginning of the school day. The novelty of having an American teacher helped to increase the number of students, which resulted in greater cooperation from the townspeople. There were only a small number of girls enrolled, as was the case in most rural schools.

The objective of the IVS project was to help train Liberian teachers in modern methods, school management and leadership skills. After working with us for one year, the teacher was to enroll in the educational leadership training program at the institute operated by Tuskegee Institute in Liberia. The IVS teacher would get a new partner, and the internship cycle would continue. After two years, our tour would be over, and we would have helped train two Liberian teacher/principals. However, the Peace Corps was established, and it ultimately replaced the IVS in Liberia. I don't know how many Liberian teachers actually completed the original program. Of the 5 teachers I helped train, only two would qualify for the institute program.

BECOMING A REAL TEACHER AND TECHNICIAN

I found that Adjo Kwabala a pleasant man to work with. He was older than me, and he was married with two children while living next to the courthouse building. I suspected that he was a little jealous of my enhanced status among the students and in the community, considering my youth and lack of experience, but he was quite professional and cooperative. In addition, he was familiar with the people and tribal authorities we needed to help with school improvements.

We began by taking an inventory of school materials and the names and addresses of the students. We reorganized the attendance record and medical information. I learned that Gbartala was one of the sites for the construction of a new government school, and we would need laborers to help with the project. USAID provided the cement, wooden pallets and the block making machine, while the town provided the sand.

I was surprised to find the students using discarded elementary school books from the San Francisco school district. The story of "Ted and Jane," taking the train to visit their grandparents, was so far from the reality of those students there in the middle of the Liberian rainforest. There were some books, written by the Lutheran Mission, being used in their schools, but Liberian school administrators choose the donated texts from America, because they wanted to expose students to modern western values and ideas.

"We are trying to raise them from the backward ideas of the tribal culture and give them a model to strive for," one superintendent announced at a district meeting.

Teachers like Adjo were just grateful to have enough books and materials and didn't protest about their origin. The textbook controversy reminded me of my courses at Hampton, but I listened, like a good novice.

I was never a solid math and science student, but I found myself trying to teach basic concepts about multiplication and division, fractions, and percentages. Students assumed I possessed unlimited knowledge on most subjects, so I carefully identified the subjects where I had specialized knowledge and emphasized that learning is a continuous process. I used anecdotes whenever possible, and that proved effective in maintaining their attention.

My most memorable and enjoyable class was one in which I demonstrated the difference between centrifugal and centripetal force, using a pail of water. The pupils were attentive and well-behaved, so I seldom had to discipline anyone. Administrators warned us to avoid any criticism of the Liberian government when teaching Social Studies.

I was delighted to find some students had heard about the conflict between white and Black American soldiers stationed in Liberia during WWII. According to some of the Americo-Liberians I conversed with, white and Black American soldiers, who were separated by race in a segregated military fought with each other about the use of equipment, recreational use, event attendance and being off base at the same time.

One of my objectives was to encourage more student participation in class, because most had been trained in "recitation and memorization." The teacher wrote on the board and asked students to read or recite, emphasizing correct pronunciation. In my classes, we discussed the different types of people in the area and how they felt about the school and modern learning. It became clear that students were impressed with grandiloquence and lofty language they heard some local adults use in court and at cafes.

There was a male nurse who had been trained in Sierra Leone and who spoke with a cultivated British accent. When plied with enough cane juice or beer, he would begin pontificating about the topic of the day, using bombastic language. Students would ask me why I didn't use expressions like "the vicissitudes of life" like Sam, the nurse? I told them that they wouldn't understand me if I spoke like that; I didn't need to show off my level of learning. Speaking in clear, simple terms that people understood was my purpose. I did tell them that increasing their vocabulary was a *good* habit, but it should not be used to impress others.

One of the textbooks contained a description of the original American Black immigrants, dubbed, "Americo-Liberians," who founded the nation of Liberia. Their hardships with the tropical untamed environment and the reaction of indigenous people along the coast were briefly explained, which we talked about in our short history unit.

When I asked my students what they thought being "civilized" meant, they said it meant "educated people and foreigners"—people who "know book." In response, I told them about an old lady from the bush who gave me a bowl of rice because I didn't have anyone to cook for me. To me, she was exhibiting a kindness that I thought represented civility, but not to my students. They insisted that tribal people in the bush were not civilized. When I asked *why?* they responded, "Teacher, she don't speak English and don't know book."

I then retorted with, "But helping a stranger is a Christian *obligation*, according to the Holy Bible." During these discussions, Adjo and some of his students seemed to be listening to us and told their parents and neighbors what "Teacher Davis" was saying. I would love to have been able to listen to those conversations.

THE BIG MEN IN GBARTALA

I soon discovered who the important townspeople were, because my house was near the most frequented places: *Vernon Reeves' Café and the courthouse. I passed through the café yard, walking home from school, and I began buying a quart bottle of Monrovia Beer and put it in my refrigerator. It wasn't long before Reeves sent his carboy to summon me to the café. Students said that he was a "big man" in town and owned two other such stores along the main highway and farms as well.

Reeves lived in Monrovia, had an important job involving imports and exports, owned an executive office building, and he knew President Tubman personally. He drove a Ford pickup truck on his trips up-country and usually was accompanied by an employee. He liked to drink liquor, usually in the company of a few other men in town who were literate. He also had local girls who worked at the café and store, and I quickly learned that they were off-limits to me.

He told me in jest, "Davis, I'm afraid you gone steal my Gbartala girls when I go back Monrovia," to which I replied, "No, I'm too busy correcting papers every night," which got laughs and guffaws. Actually, IVS teachers were warned about getting too intimate with Liberian women, betrothed or not.

It was unrealistic to expect a group of young American teachers and technicians to ignore the young women in their villages, some of whom going about with their breasts uncovered. When Kessler got word of certain teachers having relations with women, he made a point of telling us that the penalty for getting a Liberian girl pregnant was a two thousand dollar fine. I don't know if that was true or an idle threat. I can only say that I was cautious about getting involved with women, especially those girls who were betrothed to a chief or someone else.

Polygamy was common in Liberia, and certain men of means could afford to pay the bride price for multiple "wives." A chief or "Big Man" like Reeves would claim a young girl as his betrothed by meeting with her parents and paying the bride price, with the understanding that the consummation would be after she was of childbearing age.

As those girls blossomed into womanhood, they might become interested in a younger man and have intercourse with him. When her "husband" found out, he could force her to "confess" the name of the man she had slept with, who could then be fined in the local tribal court. I found out that this was a common scam. Many arguments at the local court involved charges against adulterers.

On the hill just south of the town was a gas station and farm owned by the Flemister's, an Americo-Liberian family. When I moved to Gbartala, Jimmy Flenister, his wife, Nimbya, their baby and Jimmy's father were living in the ranch house that Jimmy built. They emigrated from Chicago as followers of the Garvey Movement. Jimmy was the first to arrive in 1951, fearing that he would be drafted during the Korean War. He began building the house where he later would be joined by his parents and two siblings. His mother had died before I arrived, but I had interesting conversations with his father about America's race problem.

Jimmy's father told me that I "belonged" in Africa and that I was just realizing it. Then he asked me if I had read the major literary works by Black authors like Langston Hughes, Countee Cullen, Richard Wright, and others. When I admitted that I hadn't, he loaned me a couple books and told me that they contained more about my experience than any of the U.S. History texts I had studied. I must say that I felt quite unprepared and uncomfortable with that conversation, but Mr. Flemister was really a nice and thoughtful man who was well respected in the area.

Besides Jimmy, who was about 28, there was Helen, an older sister who was married. Helen had a young daughter and lived on a church mission compound in another province. Her former husband was a Yardley, a nephew of President Tubman. Their marriage didn't last, and she spent much of her time with her father at the farm. After she invited me to dinner and a game of scrabble, I got to know the family much better. Her other brother, Bob, was an electrician, employed by the Raymond Construction Company, which was building the railroad line from the iron ore mine site to the coast. I only saw him a couple times and found him to be quiet and reserved.

Jimmy, who was quite the opposite of William, was extroverted and aggressive. He was happy to see me come to town and informed me that his family was partly responsible for my being there, as they had urged USAID to send an American teacher to Gbartala, where they guaranteed town support for the new school project. He often dropped by my house and made himself comfortable. He liked to brag about the women he had been with and invited me to walk with him through town at night, looking for female companionship.

Many of the local girls were afraid of Jimmy, since he had literally "picked up" and carried a girl back to his house years earlier. He was big guy, about 6'7", who was loud and garrulous. However, he was generous and helpful to me, but a bit overbearing. He was also a handyman who operated their small gas station and was well-known in the area. His wife was of the Vya tribe, and they had a little baby girl. Unlike his friend, Jimmy Stewart, in nearby Gbandela, he was not fluent in the local Kpelle language.

The Paramount chief and his clerk were also among the power brokers in town. The clan controlled the land, and Liberian government officials had to cooperate with the chiefs in matters relating to road and bridge construction and land sales. I had little contact with the Paramount chief in town, except at holidays, when the school children were required to participate. I had to seek his assistance in acquiring more help with our cement block making project for the new school, but he spoke to me through an interpreter, even though he understood English and could speak it well enough to converse with anyone.

There was also a Lebanese store owner who sold most of the dry goods, canned foods, beverages, tools and practically any item one needed, like cement, lime etc. Since there was no electric power in town, except for a generator at the store and the café, my appliances and lamps required kerosene, supplied by USAID.

I was close enough to the Village of Gbandela and Stewart's restaurant to ride there on my motor bike for lunch or dinner or visit the IVS teacher, R.T. Gadison, who lived in a small trailer behind the restaurant owned by the Stewarts. Gadison had indoor plumbing and electric power, provided by the Stewart's generator. He was one of the first group of IVS teachers, previously located in Ganta District, near the border with Guinea. Like most of the original group, Gadison was older, and he had been a teacher and counselor in Louisiana. He was also the oldest of the African Americans in the group, and he was popular. He had a great sense of humor, was quite the ladies' man, and hence a concern for our leader, Kessler.

Gadison had met an officer in the Liberian Army's Frontier Force in Ganta who introduced him to educated members of the Liberian elite class in Monrovia. He became familiar with the city's nightlife and loved to share his experience with other team members. Gadison was also good enough in the kitchen to teach me how to prepare tasty meals. His pot of navy beans, pork and peppers was especially delicious. He teased me about my habit of humming while eating, and quipped, "Junebug, I'm your pal, not your *papa*," when I asked for seconds.

An elderly African American immigrant who had only recently arrived lived adjacent to the restaurant. It seemed he was an old acquaintance of Mr. Stewart who wanted to spend his last years in Africa. He lived on means provided by his Social Security check, and the Stewarts lodged him in a small house on the compound near the restaurant. I didn't really know him or much about his circumstances until he died.

Mr. Stewart's workers dug a hole for his burial, and we all gave him a nice funeral service. I was one of the pallbearers, and while lowering his simple pine casket into the grave, my pack of Pall Mall's fell into the hole. The Liberians insisted I climb down and retrieve them because it was bad luck to leave such an item in a grave; so I did just that. It was an eerie feeling climbing up out of that grave.

I had been cutting my own hair and friends' hair for years, and I did so for Gadison, Jimmy Flemister, and Jimmy Stewart, who lived with his family in the house he built. I was a little nervous trimming his hair because he suffered a terrible third degree burn years earlier that scorched most of his left ear and neck as well as his torso.

Apparently, Jimmy was visiting a girlfriend who asked him to fill the kerosene tank on her refrigerator (which contained some gasoline as well). When he lit the wick, it exploded, severely burning him over a large part of his body. He wallowed in the dirt to put out the fire, without much assistance from whomever was around. He was not expected to survive, but he did.

Jimmy became a legend among the Kpelle people for his strength, determination and his fluency with their language. I heard them say that "Jimmy speak Kpelle better than a Kpelle man self." His wife was a traditional girl, and apparently Jimmy had taken her sister as a second wife. He was a carpenter, plumber, electrician, mechanic—a guy who could fix almost any appliance. He was a small boy when his family came to Liberia, and he spent his formative years with the other boys in the area. His older sister was very attractive, was married and lived in Monrovia.

Mr. Stewart's secretary functioned as a hostess at the restaurant, the favorite eating place for Americans and others traveling up-country. She was friendly and professional while talking with the diners. When I asked about her love life, she told me about her engagement to an educated Liberian farmer who had graduated from Hampton and lived a few miles away. She said he gave her a ring, and they were planning to get married, but she insisted that his traditional wife, or concubine, and her children must move away first. He refused, saying that she could not make such a demand, so they broke up. The gossip suggested that Mr. Stewart was sleeping with his secretary and that caused the split. When I asked Gadison if he ever tried to hit on her, he laughed, saying that he didn't want Mr. Stewart as an enemy.

MY HOUSEBOY, IVS TENANT
AND BRIDGE TO THE COMMUNITY

I had been in Gbartala about 3 months when a student, Henry Cooper, and his father, a clan chief, approached me, asking if Henry could lodge with me as a houseboy while attending our school. Apparently, he had lived with another teacher or clerk earlier, and his father wanted him to live in town, away from his home in the bush. He had a letter of recommendation from his previous mentor, and I agreed.

His father promised to bring rice from his farm and other food items when he could, and he assured me that Henry was a good cook, which I discovered. He could wring a chicken's neck, de-feather it and prepare a meal. Additionally, he knew how to keep a house clean, and he was a big help in my relationship with the townspeople. He also knew how to make himself scarce when I had female company, and he told me which girls were concubines and thus off-limits.

Henry's father did not reveal to me that his son had malaria, which I learned when he got a fever and chills one night. I gave him a couple of my Quinoline pills, and he got better. USAID supplied us with this medicine, and I began giving Henry pills regularly. This kept him free of the malarial fever and chills.

As a member of a large extended family, Henry, like most traditional people, referred to several other boys and men as "brother" and to young women in town as "sister." Because he was living with me, his relatives assumed that he had access to food and kerosene and other items that they could borrow. Henry said that tribal people referred to me as a "Big Man" because of living situation, my job and my motor bike.

I was a "Kwi Quelli" to them, despite my attempt to explain otherwise. When I bought some cans of Carnation Milk for a sick woman and her baby, some neighbors said I was wasting my money since the child was going to die because the mother was evil. When I replied that this was foolish, Henry interpreted my response differently so as not to offend the neighbors. Despite having found a driver to take the child to the hospital in Gbarnga, she died anyway.

Just before I moved from Gbartala to another location, I had a confrontation with a drunken soldier in a bar in town, run by a woman who turned out to be Henry's older sister. I was having a beer there one evening when the soldier entered the place, carrying an M1 rifle. Before he sat down, he told the barmaid to bring him a beer and charge it to the Kwi Quelli, referring to me.

"Teacher, I must do so?" she asked.

"No," I said. "He should have asked me."

Then the soldier got up from his seat with the rifle and started to approach me, slurring his speech and threatening me. Instinctively, I punched him in the face, and he collapsed, the rifle falling to the floor. The barmaid begged me to leave and feared, "big trouble oh." Henry's father was able to settle the matter without me having to go to court. Fortunately, I never saw that soldier again when I went to and from Gbarnga.

Charlie Simmons, an IVS teacher, had been assigned to the village of *Gbondi, about 20 miles south of Gbartala. He was an African American veteran from North Carolina, and until his trailer was set up, he was staying with me. Charlie was having a difficult time getting adjusted to the climate and the food, so was sick often and stayed in the house on most days. It appeared that he was not a good fit for that assignment, as he was quiet, reserved and didn't mix well with the people.

At this point, I was spending a lot of time at Reeves' Café, at the Flemisters or visiting Gadison, who gave Charlie the nickname, "Mole," because he stayed inside so much. Mr. Reeves asked, "Why is Charlie so shy and doesn't come to the café for a drink?"

Eventually, Charlie moved to Zainfue, and I didn't see much of him after that. The two other Black IVS teachers, with whom I had little contact, were Ted Owens, from Boston, and Kurt Johnson from Baton Rouge. Keith had accompanied Gadison in the original group.

BUILDING BLOCKS TO A NEW SCHOOL
AND MEMORIES OF GBARTALA

Whenever I recall my time in Gbartala, I picture Reeves, sitting outside of his café with a bottle of Beck's beer, laughing and talking with a couple of local friends. One of them would say in jest, "I drink to make the malaria mosquito drunk!" I learned much local news and gossip while talking with those men who seemed to genuinely enjoy my company and appreciate my work at the school.

One day, Mr. Reeves asked me to ride with him to his farm, several miles northwest of town. He had been drinking most of the day before we left, and he drove slowly and steadily, telling me he could drive all the way back to Monrovia after consuming liquor. I told him that perhaps he should let me drive.

When we arrived at his rubber tree farm, his workers were gathered under a thatched-roof veranda, with a big table and a few chairs. It was Saturday—payday, and Reeves and his assistant checked the entries in the account book before paying each employee after deducting their purchases at his store. This was the typical country farm store operation. It was interesting to witness the interaction even though I couldn't understand most of their language. That trip gave me a clearer idea of Reeves' up-country holdings, which he said were more of a burden because of all the expenses.

USAID chose the town of Gbartala as the site for a new government school. It was to be built on the existing school compound, with help from the townspeople. After the materials were delivered to the site, I began making the cement blocks. The proper mixture of sand, cement and water was required, and this damp mortar had to be tamped into the groves of the device resting on a wooden block. When the metal template, or mold, was raised, a perfect cement block was formed, and then we set it out in the sun to dry and harden.

I spent most of my vacation making blocks instead of going on a trip or staying in Monrovia. I made over one thousand block that were used in the new school, built after IVS left Liberia. I continued this project in Palala, my new location, making at least 3,000 blocks. These buildings were 200 feet long and 40 feet wide, with corrugated zinc roofs. A new teacher's house was also to be constructed on the compound, but only two had been built during my tour.

It took me a while to learn how to hold my liquor. I had been an athlete in college and hadn't done much drinking. There in Liberia, where alcohol was cheap through the duty-free port facility for USAID employees, I could buy a case of Johnny Walker scotch for $3 a bottle. I had to keep my whiskey hidden from Jimmy Flemister, who would stop by unexpectedly and just open the refrigerator, looking for a bottle.

One night at the café, while talking and sipping with Reeves and friends, I got wasted after eating country chop with peppers. A woman helped me across the road to my house, and she ended up spending the night with me. She said that she was married and lived in Monrovia and that Reeves was giving her a ride back. She assured me that her husband would never find out about her time with me.

Another time, when Gadison and I had dinner in Monrovia at a restaurant, I got drunk from mixing beverages. We had attended a cocktail party earlier, at the home of Jimmy Stewart's older sister, who was married to a lawyer. At her urging, I had a small bowl of tripe soup, which was not compatible with the later drinks and dinner. There was always an occasion where I was pressured to try some traditional food to avoid insulting a host. I once had some country chop at the home of an agricultural extension aide, and when the hot peppers forced me to drink a glass of water that was not boiled, I got a mild case of dysentery.

IVS informed us that the contract would not be renewed because Peace Corps volunteers, training in Puerto Rico, would be arriving soon. I would be able to complete my two-year tour as an IVS teacher, but some of our recent arrivals would have to work as IVS/Peace Corps members. Peace Corps was President Kennedy's new organization, so IVS had to be discontinued. When I asked if I could stay on for another tour as a Peace Corps volunteer, Peace Corps answered that I would have to apply and take the training in Puerto Rico. I had to chuckle at this response. Peace Corps was modeled after the IVS, which had been operating in Southeast Asia and Africa since 1956.

A USAID officer brought a Peace Corps supervisor around to my house to ask me various questions about my housing and several questions about how I got my food and medical care. After I answered all his questions, he said that I would still have to undergo their training to become a volunteer. When their teachers arrived in Gbarnga, we all met for discussion, and while introducing myself, I almost said, "Gerald Davis, Peace..." because I followed several Peace Corps members. I got teased about that for a while.

CREATING A COMMUNITY OF CARE IN PALALA

I must admit that I loved living in Gbartala, because it was not as isolated as some towns, and I had become close to Gadison, the Flemisters and the Stewarts in Gbandela. Ma Stewart's country chop and pineapple upside-down cake were the best, as was the conversation with fellow African Americans. However, due to district commisioner's decision to return my house to its original function, a clinic, I had to move, or so they explained it to me.

There were no other available appropriate houses to rent in town. I suspected that there were other reasons for having to move involving me getting too intimate with local girls, or "going native." Anyway, I was relocated to the town of Palala, about 30 miles to the north, above Gbarnga, the district headquarters. Henry Cooper came along with me, with the blessings of his family.

On the day of my move, I got news from my family at home about of the death of my sister, Nancy, who had succumbed to a brain tumor, despite an operation in Kansas. Her husband, Leon Ford, was stationed there as an airman with the United States Air Force. She was a young mother with two boys, and I last saw her at her apartment in Orange, New Jersey, before I left the states. Of course, I could not return home for the funeral. It was a sad time for me, since there were no phones in my area for calling home. Ron Kessler told me to take a few days off, until I was ready to assume my duties, but I preferred to stay busy while dealing with my grief.

Palala was divided by the main north/south highway and the road to the east where the railroad construction was underway. My house was on the latter, near the divide, and my neighbors were so close that there was little privacy. Large trucks passed by regularly to and from the railroad building site. However, the new space was much larger and better than my previous dwelling.

USAID had rented it from a local rubber farmer whose father had it built it, but he died before he could move in. Built with mud blocks with a stucco outer-coating, painted white, it had large windows and shutters with screens, and a zinc roof. Two other IVS guys had lived there earlier. One was a skilled carpenter and handyman who had made some valuable improvements. He installed gutters on the front and rear of the house to collect rainwater in a 55-gallon drum, placed on a scaffold near the back door.

A hose was attached to allow running water in the kitchen sink that was built of cement, connected to an outside sewer pipe that ran to a soak pit. There was also a bathtub in the utility room off from the kitchen that also drained to the soak pit. In addition to the kitchen, there were 3 large bedrooms, a living room and a spacious front porch. The outhouse was in the backyard along with a small utility shack that I used to store tools and my motor bike.

The Palala government school was on the north end of town and was constructed with mud and sticks. It had a cement, whitewashed stucco coating, housed under a zinc roof. Like Adjo Kwabala, the principal, Mr. Ware, carried a small stick or wooden pointer to get the attention of the students and was assisted by David Bairon, who taught first through third grade.

Apparently, the principal had a habit of taking his lunch break at home, where he washed his meal down with palm wine. When the district superintendent got word of this habit, Kwabala was forced to resign. A younger, mission-trained man replaced him, and eventually a Nigerian man from Ibadan who taught math joined our staff.

There was a higher percentage of girls in the Palala school, and most of the students seemed to be better prepared for the work. Assigned to the 5th and 6th grades, I continued to emphasize reading comprehension, written communication and class discussions, some of which became very lively. Students were interested in world events, especially the Cuban missile crisis, which the *Voice of America* covered in its broadcasts across West Africa, as did *Radio Moscow*. Students were also interested in Africa's struggle against colonialism and what role Liberia played in that movement.

Some of my fellow teachers felt that I should have placed more emphasis on basic skills, but I believed those discussions were what kept several older boys coming to school daily. I knew that their parents needed them on the farms and questioned the practical value of daily schoolwork. When I gave students homework, many kids had no place at home to study or a lamp to use at night.

There was practically no privacy in their traditional thatched-roof houses. Henry reminded me how better off he was than his peers, because he had his own room, lamp, dictionary and paper to write on. One night, while we were enjoying rice, meat patties with tomato sauce, and green beans for dinner, Henry said, "You know, teacher, these kids not eating like this, they be lucky to get small bowl of rice, self."

CARE, the organization that provide food for the poor, USAID and the Liberian government cooperated to improve the nutrition for school children. If a town built a kitchen and a secure place to store items like corn meal, flour, beans, cooking oil, etc., and the town selected a person to manage it, CARE would supply those food items and instructions on how to use them. In Palala, we built a CARE kitchen and storage closet on the school compound. The daily meal prepared at the kitchen was the only real nutritious meal for many of our students, who had to walk a considerable distance to school. And the facility proved a big plus for both the school and town.

When I arrived, there was no football (soccer) field at the school compound, so that became a priority project. Using a vacant open area along the road that had been cleared of brush a year earlier, we assigned each of the bigger kids a section of the field to clear by themselves. To help move the process forward, any student who was being punished had to work it off, clearing a section of the field.

There were a few old palm trees that had to be removed, so the older boys cut them down and dug up the trunks, as well as cut and installed trees for the goal post. Eventually, we had our first game. A Nigerian teacher volunteered to coach our team. Working with IVS teachers, I arranged the games with other schools and secured help from town at transporting the team to away games. We won 3 of the 5 games we played while I was there.

The agricultural extension agent lived in town, and with his help our school started a 4-H Club and developed a nice garden behind the school. We selected a good spot with rich dark soil, and the kids cleared away the trees, roots and vines, and they prepared the spaces for planting, with ditches for irrigation. We planted tomatoes, eggplant, beans, cabbage, okra, collards, kale, sweet potatoes, cassava and carrots.

During the clearing of the site, one boy was bitten by a snake on his shoulder when I was away, but students came to get me and we took the boy to the medicine man, who treated him. One teacher said the snake was not poisonous, but the boys said it was. At any rate, the victim was able to return to school in a few days, seemingly cured. I asked the healer what he used to cure the boy, but he refused to tell me, saying I was a Kwe Quelli and wouldn't understand, according to my student interpreter.

TRUE WHIG PARTY AND OPPOSITION GROUPS

During my time at Palala, there was a national election, in which the True Whig Party, whose candidate, William Tubman, had been the president since 1944, was once again on the ballot along with his vice president. Even though there was an opponent, he only offered praise for the incumbent. Thus, no one expected him to win many votes. We were warned to keep our thoughts to ourselves about this sham democracy or risk being arrested and deported.

I learned very quickly that it was not wise to say or do anything that could be construed as disrespecting the President or his spouse. The First Lady was to attend an event in Gbarnga District, held at the central school where students typically lined the road with flowers, awaiting her arrival. Because she was noticeably late, the American teacher on the staff (not

IVS) decided to leave before she arrived. His action did not go unnoticed, resulting in his early departure, or more likely his dismissal.

The President was genuinely held in high esteem by most of the people. His National Unification policy did much to reduce the discontent among the indigenous people in the interior. Their land-owning rights were restored, and his administration appointed special provincial commissioners to protect their rights to own firearms and to have counsel in disputes and trials. The President traveled to all areas of the country, meeting with tribal leaders and building the strength of the True Whig party.

There remained, however, pockets of opposition, evidenced by an attempted *coup d'état*, staged by a faction of the army, but the president had officially forgiven the captured leader. However, rumor had it that the guy had disappeared.

I saw the President's motorcade in Monrovia once, but that's as close as I came to meeting him. During my two years in the country, I felt comfortable and free to travel wherever I wanted. The only problem I had was with soldiers who tried to extort a bribe (dash). The True Whig Party sent its representatives to all the major towns to meet with the chiefs, town clerks and schoolteachers to encourage people to vote.

In Palala, our older male students went to the local polling stations in town and voted. One 16-year-old boy said he voted 5 times. Other boys gave similar accounts of how they were allowed to cast several votes, because the officials were under pressure to use all the ballots they had been provided. I was not aware of the girls voting. It was a holiday in town and much drinking and merrymaking occurred. The incumbent president won 98 percent of the vote.

In March 1963, the Jehovah's Witnesses from many countries held their convention in Liberia. Because they refuse to swear oaths of allegiance to governments, salute flags or sing national anthems, they were persecuted by members of the Liberian Frontier Force. They were meeting in the town of Gbarnga, where one of their missionaries who was a black American in his fifties and his wife were humiliated by soldiers. I had seen him occasionally in town and conversed briefly with him.

When it became apparent that the Jehovah Witnesses would not begin their convention gatherings by saluting the Liberian flag or singing the national anthem, they faced deportation. The white female members were forced by soldiers to walk to the local creeks barefoot, carrying water pails on their heads. Males were beaten and roughed up if they refused to salute the flag. I didn't witness these actions, but it was the topic of conversation among expatriates, and Liberia was taken to task for this sorry episode by the International Organization at its next meeting in New York.

Although not a part of the opposition to the Liberian government, the Eastern European Communist technicians working in Guinea across the northern border at the iron ore mines were a worry to USAID, as well as the Liberian government. The Nimba mountains, shared with Guinea, contained some of the richest iron ore in the world. Unlike Liberia, Guinea, a former French colony, under the leadership of a socialist, had become a non-aligned state, willing to accept economic aid from Communist countries and the West. When France retaliated and withdrew all their technical people, Guinea turned to the Soviets for help.

It was common to see Czech technicians with sidearms in Ganta and Sanniquellie towns near the border. IVS had teachers and technicians in these areas, and we were warned to avoid any contact with those guys. Apparently, Liberia had allowed Guinea to transport some of its ore to the Liberian ports via the new railroad, built by LAMCO, the Liberian American Mining Company.

THE LONG REACH OF AMERICAN RACISM

W.E.B. Dubois once described the feeling of comfort, of being safe among ones' own, that he felt when he landed in Ghana. I understand that sensation, of being among my own black people, and knowing that I belong. In Liberia, I felt this way from the first day, seeing all the black Africans at the airfield and along the road to the Capital. I was almost light enough to be mistaken for a white man, but the Africans I spoke with told me that I was a brother from America and that Africa was really my home also. After all, Liberian citizenship was still restricted to persons of African descent.

Liberia was officially a black man's country—the only African nation without a colonial past. It was founded by the American Colonization Society, whose purpose was to repatriate freed Negro slaves. The original settlers lived primarily along the coast, imitating the culture of the southern planter society. Consequently, these Americo-Liberians became the ruling class of the new nation, established in 1847.

The U.S. maintained a tenuous relationship with the new nation, which it didn't formally recognize until the 1860s. During WWII, the U.S. had a military base there with American black and white troops, operating under Jim Crow policy. Liberians talked about how the white and black troops did more fighting between themselves than with the Germans. It became clear to me the degree to which anti-Black racism infected Liberian society and the Americans working there with businesses and the USAID mission.

From the first meeting between USAID officials and our group of 4 teachers, I began hearing negative criticisms about The Booker

Washington Vocational School that had been run by Black Prairie View
University educators. It was just outside Monrovia, in the town of Kakata
near the airport, when people complained to me about all their mistakes,
like wasting money, about projects that weren't completed and their
aloofness. I heard this often enough that I reacted by asking, *Why this was
only being talked about by whites?* The response—it was not customary
for Liberians to criticize foreigners.

After I became acquainted with the Flemisters and Stewarts, I began
hearing about how Liberians reacted to white racists working in Monrovia.
They talked about how Liberians were called "monkeys," "childlike" and
"ignorant" by white officials and business owners. Hence, a group of
young men would retaliate with violence. But most Liberians didn't react
overtly to rude foreigners. The Tubman official policy ignored white
foreign social attitudes as long as they remained private and were not
publicly aimed at the President or other members of the Liberian
government.

I had my own confrontation with a USAID technician on The Booker
Washington School campus. I got a ride to Monrovia with our Acting
Chief of party, Paul Kruger, and with David Strong. I forget the reason we
stopped at this individual's house; perhaps he was a friend of Klein. He
invited us in for a cold drink, and during the conversation, he began this
tirade about Prairie View ruining the school. I had never met this guy
before, but I assumed that he knew I was Black, but he said, "This is a
Texas nigger's conception of beauty," referring to a building on campus.

I was momentarily shocked, and I could see Kruger and Strong turn
crimson, so I told the guy, "If you hate Blacks this much, you shouldn't be
working in Africa." I then got up and walked out to wait for Kruger. They
tried to apologize for the guy, but I was having none of it. I told Gadison
and several others about the incident and learned that similar comments
from him were common.

I learned about another incident involving this same issue that resulted
in serious consequences for Dr. Reasoner, the same individual who
initially criticized the Prairie View University stewardship of the
vocational school. A group of American educators were visiting Liberia
and evaluating the joint educational program between the Republic of
Liberia and USAID. Apparently, Reasoner repeated his bad mouthing of
Prairie View's work and made additional negative comments about
African American attitudes toward Liberians.

One of the women in the group was recording the session and sent a
copy back to the U.S. State Department, resulting in Reasoner being
relieved of his duty and being sent home immediately. The U.S.

government was especially sensitive about these incidents, because *Radio Moscow* would report such in their broadcast throughout Africa.

Most of the foreign concessionaires in Liberia, beginning with Firestone Rubber Plantation, received valuable tax exemptions as well as freedom from government regulations. The Government of Liberia did not require these companies to place Liberians in key management positions. Africans were basically employed at the lower levels, as laborers, factory workers, truck and equipment operators, and interpreters. The only black African manager at Firestone Rubber Corporation was the supervisor of schools, for its Liberian employees. When Gadison' s two-year tour was completed, he was hired by Firestone as a supervisor in one of its rubber manufacturing plants, making him the first person of African descent to hold such a position. The company gave him a residential cottage on the plantation, a car, and guaranteed transportation to and from the U.S.

I learned about race relations at Firestone when Gadison said that Liberia's Open-Door Policy toward foreign corporations prevented the government from making serious demands related to promoting Africans to senior management positions. The changes taking place in the other newly independent African nations were beginning to have its impact on Liberia, but the presidential regime in power maintained its generous policy toward concessionaires. It was clear that many of the whites working in Liberia continued to exhibit the paternalistic and racist attitudes toward Liberians, regardless of their socio-economic class.

The political and economic power in the country was in the hands of the larger Americo-Liberian families, who were concentrated in the counties along the coast, but some had big farms and plantations up-country in the 3 provinces. The Dunbar's were one of those families that had a big farm, just north of Palala, about 3 miles back off the main road. Apparently, I looked like some of Mr. Dunbar's sons or grandsons, because on several occasions people asked me if I was a Dunbar. The patriarch emigrated from Pennsylvania and settled on Monkey Island on the coast, in Sinoe County. Intermarriage took place between Dunbar's and other families. Some of the children were of a light complexion, but most looked like the other indigenous people.

The Dunbar family farm was a big operation, according to the people in Palala. The old man Dunbar had died before I arrived, and by some accounts had fathered 102 children by over 30 different wives or concubines. Apparently, he left 3 wives pregnant upon his death. Young men were prohibited from entering the farm, because Mr. Dunbar feared they would have relations with his women. I passed the road leading to his farm, but I did not enter.

As I mentioned before, polygamy was quite common in the country, and many of the "Big Men" who were legally married and lived in the capital or other cities also had one or more concubines with children living on small farms up-country. It was truly a man's world. When I was leaving Gbartala, the clan chief and Jimmy Flemister told me that the people approved of my work at the school and wanted me to stay and make Gbartala my home. In addition to offering to build me a house, they said I could take a wife from one of the young available girls in the chiefdom. Obviously, I turned down the offer, but I was gratified anyway.

APROACHING THE END OF MY TOUR — SAYING GOODBYE TO LIBERIA

After being away from the states for just about two years, I was ready to return, yet I would miss my students, fellow IVS teachers, Gadison especially, the Flemisters and the Stewarts and friendly Liberian people, who had been kind and thoughtful during my entire stay. I think one of the teachers who told me he would be using his African family name was selected to attend the Leadership Training Institute at Voinjama, in the Western Province, to become a school principal.

A colleague who had always been very friendly was sad to see me leave. He drew a picture of the Liberian Seal, depicting Providence Island, the flag and the words, "The Love of Liberty Brought Us Here," as a gift for me. Several of my students gave me artifacts that they had made or had artisans make for me, like wooden hair picks, knives, tools, country cloth, carvings and palm-thatch fish traps.

On my last day, the whole town turned out to say goodbye. My students were crying, and it was all I could do to hold it together. The clan chief gave me a beautiful tribal gown of country cloth and two big chickens. Another villager gave me a blanket, weaved from country cloth, and the father of two students wrote my division chief in USAID a fine letter about my work at the school and in the community.

The most difficult parting was saying goodbye to 15-year-old Henry Cooper, who had been my houseboy, student and friend. He had helped me as much or more than I had helped him. Since he was concerned about his source of medicine ending, I gave him my entire supply of anti-malarial pills and sulphur pills for dysentery. I bought him a Raleigh bike so he could ride to school, and I gave him some clothes and money. I wrote a letter of recommendation for him to use in case he wanted to work for another teacher.

He had my address, as he had been writing to my sister Lorraine, and he promised to keep in touch with me. Then Henry went back to his family, and I was off to Monrovia, stopping briefly in Gbandela at Stewart's Restaurant for my last plate of country chop and pineapple upside-down cake. I said my good-byes to the Flemisters, Jimmy and his family, Mr. and Ms. Stewart and their daughter.

Associates dropped me off at the USAID trailer in Congo Town, where some American expatriates lived on the outskirts of Monrovia. I spent an overnight there, and then I picked up my plane tickets and Eurail Pass from the travel agency on Broad Street and was ready to leave the next day from Roberts Airfield on a Pan Am flight. Harmer, Roger and Phil had separate plans for leaving. Harmer traveled to Egypt and Israel before returning to the states.

Gbartala Central School, pupils and teacher, 1962

Palala students with school and CARE kitchen

Local Palala woman returning from the creek with pots and pans

Photos - Section Three

Large cotton tree near Palala town entrance

Me on front porch in Palala

Mr. and Mrs. Allen—
supportive parents of three Palala school pupils

Duda women washing clothes in the creek

My neighbors' wives make *fufu*
using a mortar and pestle – Palala

A fence/gate made with sticks and vines
to prevent goats for wandering off – Duda

Me inspecting a closet wall I made for
storing food items at the Palala schoolhouse

Palala school pupils enjoying lunch
prepared in CARE kitchen (in background)

Football (soccer) game at Palala school field

Photos - Section Three

Palala men preparing soil used to dab a new stick-built house

Photos - Section Three

Me at USAID headquarters, Zorzor
(photo by Harmer Weichel)

Village of Sukrumo, near Zorzor
(photo by Harmer Weichel)

Photos - Section Three

Poro Society "Devil" on display, Zorzor, 1962
(photo by Harmer Weichel)

Poro Society graduate, Zorzor
(photo by Harmer Weichel)

Me and my IVS colleague with our motor bikes at USAID
headquarters, Zorzor, 1962 (photo by Harmer Weichel)

Loma Tribe Poro Society "Devil" marching during President
Tubman's visit to Zorzor, 1962 (photo by Harmer Weichel)

Part Four

HOMEWARD BOUND

My flight departed at 9:00 a.m. on June 18, 1963, stopping once in Rabat, Morocco, for an hour layover before landing in Lisbon, Portugal, at 5:30 p.m. I didn't have hotel reservations, but fortunately I was directed to an inexpensive *pensione* in the city, which suited me fine considering my meager funds. My room was nicely furnished and the 3-course meals were delicious.

Having never been to Europe, I decided to walk the streets, rather than use taxis. I found the city streets clean, and many of the sidewalks were hand-laid white and black marble. However, I was surprised when groups of poor children approached me, begging tourists on the Avenue of Liberty. As poor as the people in Liberia were, I never saw beggars or was stalked was ever stalked by them. When I stopped at an outdoor café to have a beer, a man approached me, asking if I was from Mozambique. He said I looked like a fellow he used to work with there when he was in the Portuguese army.

I stayed 2 days in Lisbon and took the overnight train to Madrid, Spain. Sleeping on the train helped to save money, and I planned the rest of my inexpensive vacation with that in mind. We passed groves of olive trees in the Portuguese countryside and farmers on wagons with automobile tires, pulled by horses or mules. Although only in the country for a few days, I left with the impression that there were a lot of poor people. I wondered how Portugal could have sustained its 3 African colonies of Angola, Mozambique and Guinea. I returned to Lisbon at the end of my train tour to catch my flight back to New York.

When I arrived in Madrid the next morning, I met 3 pretty, young, white South African women who, like me, were being directed to a *pensione* by a uniformed representative. The daily cost was 175 pesetas (circa $3), which included meals. The hotel was located in the downtown district, next to the Bank of Spain, within walking distance to the National Museum, the city park and other tourist attractions.

The 3 girls wanted to go to the Flamingo dancing nightclub, and they invited me along. As we talked about our backgrounds, I challenged them to explain how the South African government's policy of Apartheid could be supported, considering its negative impact on the Black majority. They quickly responded by saying they didn't agree with Apartheid, but they couldn't change the system. They insisted that they treated Blacks with respect and asked me how Americans could justify our treatment of the

"Red Indians," and Blacks as well. I did my best to describe the movement to end Jim Crow and the positive changes achieved. Afterward, we went our separate ways.

I enjoyed a concert in the park on that Sunday afternoon, and I watched a movie in Spanish as a way to learn the language and experience it with a local audience. I had studied Spanish in high school, but I had forgotten whatever I'd learned, except for how to order a beer or cigarettes. My most memorable experience in a suburb of Madrid while attending a bullfight, where I took the subway (first time ever) to the stadium. With an excellent seat, I could see the matador's expression and the eyes of the 6 bulls slaughtered that day. It was a bloody scene. Although I took several photos, I somehow lost the roll of film before I returned to the states.

After 3 days in Madrid, I took the overnight train to Barcelona, a beautiful city on the Mediterranean coast. The Sagrada Familia tour was exhilarating; the vaults suspended 70 meters above ground, the plaster models and the pictures depicting the development of this amazing structure made the tour worthwhile. The waterfront monument to Columbus, the city stadium and Montjuic Hill were delightful experiences. I spent my last night watching the film *Westside Story* in English. It would have been great to have seen it with someone else. After a while, I was just seeing as much as I could in Spain and taking pictures.

Marseilles, France, was my next stop. Once again, I arrived at 6 a.m., not knowing where I would stay. I had done little or no planning for this trip and didn't know much about the city. After awakening as the train pulled into the station, I heard all announcements in French, as well as speech by passengers as they gathered their luggage to disembark. I wasn't in the station long before an older gentleman in a uniform approached me, asking if I had reservations for a hotel or needed assistance. I was always a little suspicious of those guys, but he seemed genuine, and off we went to another modest boarding house, or *pensione*, near the station.

I felt inadequate, trying to read the menu at a nearby restaurant, so I began the bread, wine and cheese diet, which was compatible with my budget. I bought fruit when I passed a stand, and I sat on a bench to enjoy it. When I couldn't find a menu item I wanted at one restaurant, the waiter quipped, "We don't serve hamburgers." I walked to the Notre-Dame de la Garde Catholic Basilica, which was situated on the highest point in the city. It was quite a hike up there and back.

I also visited the old port of Marseilles, but the most enjoyable thing I recall about that day was swimming at a spot where others were diving in the clear water of the Mediterranean. I could see the bottom, or floor of the bay, but couldn't reach it. After I exhausted myself swimming, I stretched out on the rocks to relax and fell asleep, awakening to a serious sunburn and the realization of how vulnerable I was, sleeping with no one to watch my things. I concluded that I had to maintain a level of trust in order to enjoy myself.

My next stop was Nice, a resort city on the Mediterranean Sea, with pebble-covered beaches instead of sand, where I only spent one night. Afterward, it was on to Milan, Italy, where I had a compartment all to myself for a while, so I stretched out on the 3 seats and slept. During the excursion, the train made stops along the way to pick up and drop off passengers.

Upon arrival, I awoke at dawn to the strong smell of garlic and cigarettes from passengers entering my compartment and nudging me to sit up with the greeting, "Buongiorno!" Some passengers asked if I was an "Americano" And most seemed very friendly. One priest showed me the poster on a utility pole with the words, "Viva le Kennedy." President John F. Kennedy had toured Europe and was quite popular after his Berlin speech and the Cuban Missile Crisis. I took notice of similar posters throughout the rest of my trip in Southern Europe.

Once again, after entering the train station in Milan, an older man in a uniform approached me and offered to show me to a hotel. I agreed to his offer. When I told him I was from New Jersey, he said he was familiar with New York and had worked at Knickerbocker Brewery, which was located there. He asked me if I had visited the *gambio*, or money exchange counter, to trade some dollars for lira. I hadn't, so I left my bag with him and walked back to the *gambio*, all the while continuing to look back at him, realizing that my bag contained my return plane ticket and my passport.

He was waiting at that same place after I exchanged my money and returned, and I felt ashamed for my lack of trust in this nice man, who was there to help novice travelers like me. Since I always requested a hotel within walking distance to the station, he found a nice one that fit my budget.

Milan was considered the money and business capital of Italy, and from what I was able to see during my brief 3-day visit, it certainly looked every bit the bustling business center. I walked through the large square at the massive Cathedral of Santa Maria Nascente, referred to as "Il Duomo." The church, built in the Gothic style, held 40,000 people. Its large stained-glass windows, the numerous carved stone pinnacles and the marble statues immediately caught my eye as I approached the cathedral. I walked through the Galleria Vittorio Emanuele II, which contained many small shops and cafes, and I stopped for an espresso, which I found too strong for my taste.

I toured the Gothic church, Santa Maria delle Grazie, and I saw the damaged painting of *The Last Supper* by Leonardo da Vinci. The other memorable tour was the grand opera house, Teatro alla Scala.

My hotel did not serve meals, so I took my meals on the tours when there was time. I also discovered an American restaurant that served hamburgers, hotdogs, grilled cheese sandwiches and pizza. The guy who showed me to the hotel mentioned the restaurant in passing as a place where I could find American-style meals. I took the bus tour to Lake Como and Lecco up north, where Italians who could afford it sought refuge from the hustle and bustle of the city. Locals told us that the water temperature was too low for swimming at that time, though swimming was not a part of the tour.

Rome, my next destination, was another overnight on the train. By that time, I had become accustomed to the smell of garlic, which when combined with ladies' perfume, continued to be unsettling at dawn as passengers boarded and entered my compartment, requiring me to sit up. At the *pensione* near the train station, there was a young American Air Force veteran who was discharged and on his way home after a week's stay in Rome. He volunteered to show me some of the sites he had checked out, like St. Peter's Basilica at Vatican City, Fiumi Fountain and the Colosseum.

There were crowds of tourists and visitors at all the aforementioned attractions, especially St. Peter's Basilica. It was impossible to take a photo without someone getting in the picture. I met several Americans at those sites—some readily identifiable by language, apparel and aggressive behavior. One boorish, redheaded mid-westerner embarrassed himself by asking the tour guide where he learned to speak English so fluently. Another man I had seen in line at the money exchange was speaking loudly about how he could retire over there with his Social Security earnings.

Having just left Liberia, where poverty and illiteracy were rampant, I was especially cognizant of the affluence Americans and Europeans took for granted. After seeing several popular places on the tourist trail, I had become a little weary with the crowds and the realization that I needed much more time and money to take in all that famous city had to offer. It would also have been better to share it with some familiar company.

At the Colosseum, the traffic was horrendous. Attempting to cross several lanes of speeding cars to get close to the amphitheater was scary, because the taxi-drivers would not stop for pedestrians, or when they did, they would yell something profane in Italian, like, *"Stupido!"* To really enjoy that historic place, I needed to be inside imagining the sadistic games and torture that entertained the royalty and the plebeians.

The veteran showing me around wanted me to be sure to see the prostitutes that were situated along the side streets, near the station. They seemed older, heavier, with too much makeup, standing on the corners, shouting and gesturing with their fingers. "Come on, you know you want it." It was both scary and comical. I also observed the preponderance of small cars of different shapes and colors, a contrast to the large flashy American sedans of that time. One American, commenting on the narrow streets, wondered aloud how he could "drive his 4-door sedan down one of these streets."

I had traveled as far east as I would go. My next train ride would be a long one back to Cannes, France, where I spent one night before heading back to Barcelona. Poster signs reading *Vive La Kennedy*" were on the utility poles all along the Riviera. After checking my last book of American Express Traveler's checks, I knew that I could not afford to stay any longer than my original plan allowed. I stopped again for one more day in Madrid, and then I went back to Lisbon on the Lusitania Express overnight train.

By that time I was a little tired of walking the streets and living on bread, cheese and wine. I was ready to board the plane to return home. I had enough pesetas and escudos for a nice dinner in Madrid and Lisbon, respectively. I didn't want to be stuck with a pocket full of coins that I couldn't spend back home, but I still ended up with coins from the 4 countries.

"HOME SWEET HOME"—RETURN TO SCOTCH PLAINS

My flight from Lisbon to New York was smooth, and I made my connections at the Port Authority for a bus ride to Newark's Penn Station, where my father was waiting. It was good to be back on American soil and to see my family. Everyone was glad to see me and to hear about my experiences in Liberia and my travels through Europe. During my last months in Liberia, I had applied to 3 graduate-level degree programs in Foreign Service and International Relations.

I had hoped to win a fellowship based on my two years of grassroots experience in Liberia, but I didn't get the fellowship. Acceptance letters came from Columbia University and the Johns Hopkins School of Advanced International Studies (SAIS). I decided to matriculate at SAIS, located in Washington, D. C. My father's sister, Sally Ramsey, and her husband offered to let me stay with them.

Several changes had occurred on the home front while I was abroad. After Nancy's death, Mom began taking care of her two boys, Cornell and Tony. Their father, Leon Ford, eventually remarried, and the boys went back with him. That could not have been easy for Mom and Dad, who had two young daughters, Lorraine and JoAnn, still at home. Joe and his wife had divorced without any children, and he later married Shirley Riley, and they had a son, Joe Dee. They lived at home until he bought a house in Plainfield. George ("Danny") had married also, and he and his wife, Phyllis Pernell, who was expecting a baby, had an apartment in Plainfield.

In July, I spent some time visiting relatives, taking Mom and my sisters, Lorraine and JoAnn, to see our cousin, Nancy. She was still driving her old Chevy, and her husband and son were there at the house and glad to see us. I also went back to Washington to see Aunt Sally and family and finalized arrangements for the fall semester at SAIS.

Their son, who was working at Hotshoppes restaurant in the district as a chef, was home, and he baked a delicious coconut cream cake for us. Their daughter, Linda, who was newly married to first lieutenant Wilmer Fitzgerald, was at home as well. I agreed to accompany her to Fort Bragg, North Carolina, to pick up her husband.

When we arrived at the base, I slept in Wilmer's bunk while he went to a motel with his wife. After I had fallen asleep, some of his buddies came in the barracks and grabbed my mattress and dumped me on the floor. Before I could protest, they claimed they thought Wilmer was in the bunk. After a few laughs, I tried to sleep.

The next day, we drove to Chatham, Wilmer's hometown, where our fathers were childhood friends, and we spent an overnight. The Davis family homestead was about 4 miles from the Fitzgerald's. Wilmer Sr. was growing two acres of tobacco on our land, and he paid Daddy $400 after he sold the crop in Danville later that summer. Mr. Fitzgerald had two farms: one located on Route 57, about 4 miles west of Chatham; and a larger property further west on the same road. He was mating a mare with a roan stallion, something I had never seen before. There were no women or girls allowed at the site, even though he had 5 daughters.

We drove over to the Davis farm on Route 6 (later changed to Irish Road) to see Uncle Acie and his family. He was younger than my father and Sally, and he and his wife had remained on the homestead. They had 7 children and lived in the old farmhouse and were surprised and delighted to see us. Since we didn't have much time to linger, I took several pictures of the family, the house and the tobacco.

Only 5 of the nearly 120 acres were cleared; 3 were planted with tobacco, corn and sorghum. Uncle Acie cut pulpwood and hardwood logs to support his family. At one point, the property was put up for auction, resulting from financial issues. So after my Daddy was notified of this state of affairs, he and my brother Joe came down and stopped the auction. They were able to secure ownership of the property and ultimately had a new deed of trust drawn up, giving Daddy control of the property. I was in my junior year at Hampton and knew little to nothing about that at the time.

THE CIVIL RIGHTS TURMOIL OF 1963-64

We were in Chatham during the time that Black Danvillians were protesting against the racial segregationist policy of the city government. Danville, the last capital of the Confederacy, had remained a thoroughly-segregated city, with African Americans in no significant public positions. Notwithstanding, the 1954 Brown v. Board of Education Decision calling for desegregation "with all deliberate speed," Danville had done little to comply. I must admit that we heard little about this protest during our brief visit, nor did we experience any discrimination at the places we stopped for gas or refreshments. That was also the time of the famous March on Washington and Dr. Martin Luther King's I HAVE A DREAM speech.

It would take another year before the Civil Rights Act of 1964 was passed and *de jure* segregation in public accommodations were outlawed, but many businesses were beginning to change. I was not in a position to truly experience the ugliness and violence taking place, but I heard about the incidents on television. I heard about police brutality against peaceful Black protestors in Birmingham, Alabama, on the radio while in Liberia. Radio Moscow aired all those stories in its broadcasts throughout Africa.

The Freedom Rides and fire-bombing of the bus, the attack on the riders by angry mobs, and Malcolm X and the Nation of Islam's condemnation of American racism topped the news from America. I was absorbing all this news at the point in my life when I was trying to determine whether my career would be in the foreign service or as a teacher here in the U.S.

I was not associated at that time with any organization that was involved in the Civil Rights struggle because my focus was on getting a master's degree in International Relations. I had enjoyed my work in Liberia and seriously considered going abroad again.

When I returned home after visiting relatives and friends, there was little time to find a regular job, but I was able to make some money doing odd jobs, like cleaning up at a funeral home, bartending and landscaping. I was sure that I would be strapped for cash while attending SAIS, and I knew that I would need help from Dad, who had made it clear that he thought I would be making money at this point rather than incurring more debt. I got the same impressions from Aunt Sally, even though she welcomed me to stay with them free of charge.

Mom had banked my monthly checks from IVS, but it was not sufficient to cover my tuition and other costs. My attempts to get student aid at SAIS failed, so I was on my own. I also was without my own source of transportation, having given my Studebaker away when a senior at Hampton. It was an uncomfortable adjustment, using public buses and taxis. I didn't like standing at bus stops, waiting for the bus in the rain or cold. I guess it conjured up memories of the time I was attacked in Plainfield.

LIVING IN WASHINGTON D. C.

I felt comfortable and at home being back in Washington. I had spent a few weekends with old the Ramseys when I accompanied Miss Grobes to golf tournaments held in the area. In those days, their older sons were practically adults and spent the majority of the time away from home. They left the house via the basement door and disappeared through the alley. The youngest was closer to my age, and we spent time exploring the neighborhood. One time, when we walked to Florida Avenue and U street to a movie, we were chased all the way back home by some guys.

At breakfast, Aunt Sally and her daughter would fix a big breakfast of scrambled eggs, bacon, sausages, toast, juice and coffee. We all sat at the table and ate. At my home, there was never enough room for everyone to sit and eat together. As a finicky eater, I didn't like soft scrambled eggs, which must have irked my hosts.

Uncle Shirley worked in the maintenance department at the General Accounting Office and had his own taxicab, and Aunt Sally was a part-time nurse, specializing in the care of infants. They moved from First Street to Fifth and Farragut Street, N.W., a safer neighborhood of row-houses with larger yards. The house was also closer to the district line and Silver Spring, Maryland. Howard University, on Georgia Avenue, was not far away, and their neighbors were a mix of whites and Blacks. I could take the bus to SAIS from Fifth Street to Logan Circle and board another bus to Dupont Circle.

SAIS was a 6-story building, and many important government officials (especially foreign affairs experts) visited the school or actually taught classes there. It was a completely different environment for me after having lived in the west African bush country with poor indigenous people. Life was simple there, dress was casual, and I was more independent. In Washington, the nation's capital, life was fast-paced, hectic, impersonal and abrasive, which was a big adjustment to make.

I was majoring in International Relations and African Affairs while aiming to attain a master's degree. I learned, however, that all students were required to reach a level of fluency in a foreign language in order to graduate. So I had to take French, taught by a nice friendly lady. From the beginning, I knew it would be my biggest challenge. My other courses included African Economic Development, International Law and International Relations. I arrived at school an hour before my first class and left at 3:30 p.m. Classes were 90 minutes, and some were conducted by teaching fellows who were in the Ph.D. program.

I had to get used to lectures, taking notes and spending time with individuals who made me uncomfortable. My professor for International Law was an older man past his prime, who seemed to fall asleep occasionally. He assigned much of the teaching to his graduate assistant. *Dr. Tolbert Cooper taught one of my courses on West Africa, and he was my faculty advisor.

I got a part-time job as a receptionist in the lobby, where I was able to do some of my homework. The only student I became friendly with was a Cameroonian who was in my class on West Africa, and he was very sharp, articulate and sociable. He was fluent in French, German, Spanish and English. There were other African American students I met, both Howard University graduates. Many of the other students were from affluent backgrounds, so some went to New York on the weekends to see Broadway plays or do something else entertaining. I began to feel out-of-place, and it affected my attitude. When I compared the superficiality of student life with the meaningful work I was doing in Liberia, I doubted that I would finish the degree program.

On November 22, 1963, I decided to work on a term paper in the library on the 6th floor. When I got tired, I took the elevator to the student lounge in the basement. The television was on, and the commentator was saying, "President Johnson is boarding Air Force One." I took a seat and listened to the sad news of the assassination of President Kennedy. Like everyone at school and in the city, I was numb and overcome by grief. When I got on the bus, the mood was somber. Both male and female passengers were crying.

At Aunt Sally's house, they were watching the events in Dallas unfold and commenting. It was hard to concentrate on anything else during that time. The weather turned gloomy and cold to seemingly reflect the ambience of the city. President Kennedy's body was returned to Washington and lay "in state" at the Capitol. Like thousands of other residents, we stood in the cold, watching the funeral cortege and the president's young son saluting the casket as it passed on its way to Arlington National Cemetery.

Cousin David and I tried to view the casket in the Capitol Rotunda, but the lines were too long. The assassination shock was soon followed by the murder of the accused assassin, Lee Harvey Oswald, shot by Jack Ruby, a little-known figure associated with the Dallas underworld. Thus began the endless investigation of that tragedy, which outlived the Warren Report, confirming Oswald as the assassin.

Since I was close enough to Howard University, I often walked down Georgia Avenue to the campus. It brought back memories of my times on the football and swimming teams, competing with Howard. The Moorland Spingarn Research Center at Howard was the repository for all the printed material related to the African and African American experience.

I spent hours there, doing research for my courses. It felt great to be in the company of other scholars who were researching those priceless volumes. I found a wealth of information on ancient African civilizations in the sub-Saharan Savannah region. I was surprised and immensely proud that these sources were at Howard, the "capstone" of African American higher education.

At Howard, I felt that same sense of comfort—that ambiance of familiarity that comes with being in the presence of the African diaspora. At SAIS, I sometimes felt that I was "walking on eggshells." In one instance, my discomfort surfaced when I was invited to play Bridge, and I reacted by saying that I never learned to play *bourgeois* games. At another time, when asked why I was so bitter, I responded, "Because my grandmother was raped by a white man." As that feeling of alienation set in, I began spending more time at the Moorland Center, which was closer to home.

Aunt Sally and family were members of Vermont Avenue Baptist Church, where Dr. Martin L. King Jr., his father, Daddy King, and other SCLC (Southern Christian Leadership Conference) leaders spoke one evening. It was a privilege being in the audience and feeling the enthusiasm and hope generated by one notable speaker after another. In the rear of the audience were whites who had donated generously to the movement. They were asked to stand and be recognized.

A group of young civil rights frontline protestors, fresh-off-the-bus from Alabama, filed in to loud applause. Among the speakers were Andrew Young, Ralph Abernathy and Wyatt Walker. However, I was more attentive to Daddy King's remarks, which were designed to get the audience fired-up. He had the reputation of being more militant than his son, MLK Jr., and his words didn't disappoint.

Daddy King mentioned a litany of stereotypes that plagued Black folk, which he blamed on their white masters during slavery and the era of Jim Crow. "If they say we are lazy, you tell em they made us work for nothing, under the lash of the whip; if they say we like to steal, you tell em they encouraged this by leaving coins around for house slaves and poorly-paid servants. If they say we're immoral, you tell em they taught us that by raping our girls and mothers."

Martin L. King, Jr. spoke in more measured and deliberate words of hope. He was clearly addressing the wider national audience by encouraging Blacks to not lose hope and remain loyal to the principles of non-violence and urging whites to take a stand against racism in their own communities and workplaces. I had little money in my wallet, but I managed to put $2.00 in the collection basket. I left that event with a renewed sense of pride as an African American and hope for the future of America.

I was never comfortable with my financial situation, being dependent on the generosity of the Ramseys, who treated me like a family member and never asked for any money. They included me in all family activities and short trips. I tried my best to contribute whenever I could, buying food and other items for the house. When Christmas season arrived, I got a job at the National Post Office on First Street.

For my postal warehouse job, I had to get up early and stand in the cold waiting for the bus. Once at work, I moved packages that came down a big chute. It was hard work, and I was tired by the time I returned home However, I enjoyed the entire experience at the job and riding the bus. It was a reminder of what the 9-to-5 workday was like and an extra motivation to pursue my professional goals.

After my last day of work, I arranged to go home to N.J. to see my family for a few days before SAIS classes resumed in January. I took a Greyhound bus and sat next to an attractive young Black woman who was wearing a hijab. She was a member of the Nation of Islam and showed me her gold ring with the star and crescent, which she kept hidden by a glove.

While she was apprehensive and nervous about others seeing the ring or hearing our conversation, I expressed my admiration of Malcolm X and his message. She then encouraged me to come to the mosque on New Jersey Avenue, but I never did. Judging from the whispered tone of her remarks, I sensed that a cult-like ambience permeated the mosque and its activities.

FINDING A JOB
AND A PARTNER FOR LIFE

After returning to Washington, I received a letter from Mount Hermon School in Massachusetts, asking if I might be interested in a position in their History Department. Mount Hermon informed me that I had been recommended by Hampton Institute, after the prep school contacted them. Mount Hermon's dean of faculty invited me to an interview and asked for my resume. He paid for my bus fare, and I arrived on the campus on February 29, 1964. It was my first time in New England, and I liked what I saw and heard. I met Arthur Kiendl, the headmaster, Dr. Howard Jones, the President, Fred Torrey, the dean of faculty, Fred Bauer, the History Department Chairman and many others during my overnight on campus. After I returned to SAIS, I received a Letter of Contract, offering me the job, which I accepted immediately.

I would be teaching 4 classes in U.S. History, serving as a dormitory parent, and coaching football, swimming and golf. It was the answer to my prayers because my application for a scholarship at SAIS was rejected. I could then see light at the end of the tunnel. I knew by then that I would have had a difficult time completing the M.A. program, considering my problems in French. Also, the thought of having to board for another year with relatives and not having a car was not appealing.

I had to take two buses to get back up to Farragut Street; one from Dupont Circle to Logan Circle, where I took the J6 bus to Farragut and Fifth streets. During winter, it was practically dark by the time I got to Logan Circle, where I had to wait for 15 or 20 minutes for the bus. Sometimes, there were others at the bus stop, but not always. One night while waiting along with an elderly Black lady, a group of young Black teens came along and stopped before they reached the place where I stood. The lady advised me to be careful, because "these kid are up to no good!" I began thinking of my bad experience in Plainfield years earlier, but I was resigned to stay there and catch the bus.

One of the boys, who was about 14 or 15, walked over and asked me if I had any cigarettes. I was wearing a dark trench coat, a hat and leather gloves, holding my briefcase and wondering what was about to happen. I put my free hand inside my coat and asked him, "What brand do you want?" pretending to have a gun. The lady told them they better leave me alone, and apparently my bluff worked. The leader returned to his gang, and they walked off in another direction.

During one warm late afternoon in spring while waiting for the bus at Logan Circle, a young, attractive Black woman in a neat dress suit came around the corner and asked, "Are you Jerry Davis?" I immediately recognized her as Gale Reid, from Columbus, Georgia. She was related to a family in Scotch Plains, where her mother grew up and spent time in the summer with Gale and her sisters.

Gale was a Howard University student on her way back to the campus from a part-time job at a dentist's office. We talked briefly before my bus arrived, and I agreed to contact her at another time. When I tried to contact her, I was unsuccessful. I learned later that she had left Howard and returned home. I saw her again in Scotch Plains in July, where we became acquainted and ultimately, I asked her to marry me.

I finished classes at SAIS, packed my bags and a good friend drove up to Washington D.C. to bring me home. It was good to have a chance to talk to him about how things were going with his wife and children. Then when he told me about his affair with another woman, I cautioned him, but my advice came too late, because she became pregnant, and my friend faced the prospect of second child. I thought about the girls I had been intimate with and how I had managed to avoid becoming a "Daddy," especially during my two years in Liberia.

It was good to reconnect with my family and neighbors and hear all the gossip I'd missed during the last year. Daddy was still working on some construction site and Mom was keeping the home front together and raising two daughters. I slept in my old room on the second floor, which was Aunt Jenny's room until she died. Daddy had installed a new furnace in the basement, but everything else had remained the same. Joe and Shirley and their young family had moved into a house in Plainfield.

I immediately began looking for a job to tide me over until I started my position at Mount Hermon because I was broke, after a year at SAIS. I followed Daddy's advice and took the first job I was offered, delivering, and installing small, above-ground swimming pools. When that job didn't work out, I found a job at a foundry in Middlesex, which was a longer commute than I wanted. My job was to shovel sand on the iron molds while avoiding the hot molten pig-iron that could burn a hole through leather shoes. It was a miserable job, and I only lasted two days.

A window shade company advertised for an employee who was willing to learn the trade, so I took that job. My boss, Manni, was a nice guy whose wife also worked in the shop, making shades with her sewing machine. His teenaged daughter helped out occasionally after school. What I recall about her was that it was the summer of the Beatles invasion of America, and she screamed every time disc-jockeys played their songs. I pretended not being irritated and went about my job, delivering and installing shades and venetian blinds to customers in the area.

Since Manni had lost his business partner, and after he became pleased with my work, he offered to make me a partner for $3,000, but I declined. I never told him about my experience as a teacher abroad because he never asked for a resume. I tried hard not to talk about my education and experience, because I had no intention of continuing to work at the company after September.

Manni told me he was pleased with my work and wished I would talk more about myself. To this I chuckled, proud that I could keep silent about my education. When it was time for me to leave for Mount Hermon School, I told Manni that I had been offered a better job at a steel factory, making more than he could afford to pay me. He agreed that he couldn't match union wages and wished me well.

THE URBAN UPRISINGS OF 1964

Black people in Plainfield, Elizabeth, Jersey City and Newark, were watching the riots erupting in cities across the eastern seaboard, like St. Augustine, Florida, New York City, Cambridge, Maryland, and Rochester, New York, while sitting on their own tinderbox of racial discontent. The 1964 Civil Rights Act passed in June, banning discrimination based on race, color, religion, sex or national origin in public accommodations, sparked sit-in protests in cafes, restaurants, and hotels, where discriminatory policies continued.

The evening television network news was dominated by stories and videos of angry Blacks and whites and police brutality. When a 15-year-old Black youth named James Powell was shot and killed by a New York police officer, Harlem residents took to the streets, beginning a 6-day protest that left one dead, 118 injured, and over 400 arrested.

At the west end of Plainfield, some guys, armed with a BAR machine gun, began shooting down West Fourth Street. It's not clear about what precipitated that incident, giving rise to days of rioting and property damage.

A white policeman was killed by a mob after he shot a Black looter. Several white-owned businesses in the black community were torched. I remember driving home from work on Front Street and hoping to avoid the rioting that occurred mainly during the evenings. Years later, many torched buildings remained boarded-up, giving the appearance of a war zone. This was true for most cities where riots occurred.

A CAR, A CAREER AND A SPECIAL ENGAGEMENT

One afternoon, my sister, Lorraine, brought Diane Reid by the house. Even though their father, who was a doctor, did not come, her mother and sister Gale, whom I had met in Washington, accompanied her. I was aware they were visiting their grandmother in town while vacationing, because I used to work delivering newspapers with their cousins. On the next visit, Diane brought her sister Gale over, and after enjoying some blackberry dumplings my mother made, I invited Gale out for a drive that night, in my own car!

In preparation for my new career in Massachusetts, I purchased a 1953 Plymouth from a private owner in Westfield, NJ, which I would use for work and my date. It was good to have my own wheels again, even though the car was plain and needed some repairs. With my dad's help, we replaced the muffler and tailpipe, and it was ready for the trip up to Massachusetts in September, but for the time being, I used it for my dates with Gale, who asked me to show my color slides of Liberia to her family the next evening. I probably showed too many, but we went out later for a snack and spent time playing miniature golf and other games before we ended up necking while parked in my driveway.

Gale and I really enjoyed each other, and I was more than smitten. I was in love and so was Gale. One day later, I bought her an engagement ring and asked her to marry me. She said "yes," but we agreed to wait until she finished college before "tying the knot." Her mother was a little suspicious of my motives until Gale showed her the ring.

Since they had to leave the following day for Buffalo, New York, to visit Mrs. Reid's sister, I did not see Gale again until I visited her at Christmas in Columbus, Georgia. While there, I asked her father for her hand in marriage. Both our families were surprised by our sudden engagement. My father and brothers teased me about it in their traditional way, and Gale's father told me he had hoped she would pursue graduate work before marriage. However, both Gale and I were convinced that we were meant for each other and were determined to get married.

I drove up to Mount Hermon School before Labor Day and inspected my apartment on 3rd North Crossley. It was the largest dormitory on campus that housed junior and senior boys. The 3 faculty apartments were on the north end of the building, and each consisted of 3 rooms, including a kitchen and bathroom. There were 32 students on each floor, and we were the advisors to the boys. Among my group were several members of the varsity football team. I was just about 10 years older than most of them, and I had some in my classes as well.

Only 3 of my boys were African Americans, Ray Ramsey and Rodney Edwards, from Alabama, and Lonnie Crews from Harlem. There was a student leader on each floor who was responsible for the decorum on the floor and taking nightly bed checks, given to the faculty advisor. My floor leader was Tim Shiavoni, a varsity football player and a responsible fellow.

I was not only the sole Black faculty member, but also the only Black adult employee on campus. About 10 years earlier, a Haitian taught French for a year, so I was not the first Black to teach there or be there. As a matter of fact, a Black man had been the manager of the school laundry in the 1920s. Mount Hermon was proud of its commitment to diversity.

Throughout the school's history, there were a small number of Black
and Native American students. The same was true for its sister school,
Northfield School for girls, which was about 4 miles away, near the
Vermont and New Hampshire borders. Ann Forrester was a Black
graduate of Northfield who was teaching there when I arrived, but we
didn't see much of each other.

Both schools were part of the same corporation, with its administration
building close to the Northfield campus. Both had a long relationship with
Hampton, Howard and a few other Black colleges, which were sources for
some of their Black students. The faculty at these historically Black
institutions, located in racially segregated southern communities, sent their
children north to receive a quality education. Over the years, the children
of a few Black celebrities also attended.

I was hired to teach, coach, and advise my dorm wards, but I soon
found out that I would be asked to contribute in other ways. The school
barber could cut any type of hair, but some of the Black students didn't
like his trim ups. I had been cutting hair for years, so I gave a few free
haircuts to those who asked me.

Cutting hair brought me closer to a growing number of Black students
who felt a little homesick and needed to talk to someone about their
feelings in that predominately white community. Not long after, the school
invited me to participate in a committee to recruit more minority teachers
for independent schools. The committee met at The Choate School in
Wallingford, Connecticut, to form a plan of action.

Eventually, I travelled to a few colleges to speak with interested
minority candidates. There was a student jazz quartet called the Hermon
Knights, and I became one of their advisers. It was an interracial group,
with members on both campuses, and they cut a few records. Like most of
my colleagues, I was working 7 days a week. My only real free time was
Sunday morning, and I was invited to teach Sunday school, I declined. I
took my meals in the dining hall like other bachelors, and at lunch, each
faculty member sat at a specific table with students and a senior table head.
At breakfast and dinner, we sat wherever we wanted to.

On my first day of class, I was sharpening my pencils in the corridor,
when Tommy Donavon, the legendary English teacher, and whose classes
were across the hall from mine, came over to me and said, "You just go in
there and let them know that you are in charge." I tried to do just that. I
had learned much about class management from practice teaching at
Phenix High, and from my two years in Liberia. Mount Hermon students
were highly motivated, talented and bound for college, so I knew I was
facing a daunting challenge.

I was the youngest teacher in the department, and the books I agreed to use were as new to me as to my students. I followed my study methods from college by reading and taking elaborate notes and posing questions for discussion and others for quizzes. I wrote my objective for each class on the board and tried to accomplish it before the end of class. I gave a few quizzes, unit tests, and assigned 750-word essays.

However, I was surprised and delighted by the freedom I had to use other materials and methods in class. There was no department exam for regular U.S. History sections, taught by several teachers. The U.S. History Lecture Course, involving 4 teachers (including the department chairman) used a common exam. The class was taught like a college-level course, with visiting professors giving lectures to the combined classes.

Eventually, I felt confident enough to give two lectures. One was on "Jeffersonian Republicans," and another on "The Rise of Organized Labor." Fred Bauer sat in on a couple of my classes and met with me later to discuss his observations and offer suggestions. He was supportive and told me I was doing great.

My department had great comradery, and the advisor was also helpful when I had questions. I soon discovered that other departments did not have the same degree of cooperation. One day, while sitting in Beveridge faculty lounge, Tommy Donovan and Bill Hawley, both English department senior teachers, got into a serious argument about a committee meeting that Hawley didn't attend. When Myers threatened to report Hawley to the dean of faculty, I sat quietly, pretending to be preoccupied with my reading.

I mentioned that I had been a varsity football player and swimmer at Hampton and that I was also a good golfer when I applied for the job. In the fall, the school assigned me to the JV football coaching staff. In the winter, I joined the swimming team staff. I was supposed to help coach golf in the spring, but I was relieved of that responsibility so I could develop a new course on African studies, as there were no courses on African or African American history or literature at the school.

While perusing the library to find materials for my courses, I discovered that the school had only a few credible sources, including reference materials, so I began drawing up a list of current sources that my future classes and others would use. I discovered a collection of African artifacts in a closet in the History department, and I was able to use these items, including real iron and brass ankle-shackles from the slave trade. There was also an envelope with black and white photos of a Massachusetts congressman's visit to Liberia, showing some of the towns and villages where I had taught classes.

As a new young faculty member, several colleagues invited me to dinner. Everyone was incredibly nice and helpful. Some of these gestures may have been motivated both by curiosity and standard community protocol. Most faculty members were sophisticated when talking about racial issues, but some of the staff employees who lived in the surrounding towns occasionally expressed standard prejudices against Jews, Poles, Puerto Ricans and Blacks.

The janitor for Beveridge Hall classroom building once commented that he was, "Working harder than a nigger maid," when speaking to another worker. When I walked into the kitchen, he quickly and with great embarrassment corrected himself by substituting the words "colored maid." I was not part of the conversation and pretended I didn't hear him.

I heard several derogatory Polish jokes in both the teacher's lounge and the coach's locker room, but generally not in my presence. When a Black professor spoke to an all-school assembly, I recall hearing, "Oh he is so articulate," from a female faculty member during the coffee hour following the talk, as if she expected him to speak in Ebonics.

The headmaster made it clear that he was a liberal and that his office stood firmly behind the school's commitment to diversity. When he was a dean at Dartmouth College in Hanover, New Hampshire, his commitment regarding social changes taking place in the 1960s were the same. At the first faculty meeting, he firmly indicated that he was not comfortable with the traditional snobbish aura at some prep schools, and that Mount Hermon was embracing the move toward diversity and change, while continuing its commitment to academic excellence.

He described the minority student recruitment program, A Better Chance (ABC), founded in Boston in 1963. He insisted that Mount Hermon was a cooperating school that accepted a small number of these qualified Black students. He urged the faculty to give these students the same dedication and love that all our students and parents expect from Mount Hermon.

One manifestation of this commitment to diversity was the new Senior Faculty Forum, a series of evening lectures given by professors, government officials and civil rights pioneers. The program was limited to the Senior Class and the faculty who attended these talks in the evening. The canon of the Episcopal church spoke about the role of the church in the civil rights struggle, emphasizing Jesus's interest in the poor, marginal folk in society.

The other speaker was a Harvard Law student, who came in place of Bob Moses, the Civil Rights icon who had been arrested in Mississippi for helping register Black voters. That fellow worked in the Mississippi Summer program, and he described how local white registrars prevented eligible Blacks from voting, requiring them to read a passage from the state constitution. He described how illiterate whites were registered without any problem, while Black schoolteachers and other professionals were rejected from registering and voting.

The law student said he couldn't believe such a practice was allowed in America and spoke with such conviction about the work and sacrifice of Moses and the other leaders. He concluded that they were really in a war zone. He said that he feared for his life while in Mississippi. Since I had several seniors in my classes, we talked about that issue the following day, and I shared some of my experiences at Hampton during our boycott of local businesses that practiced Jim Crow policies.

LEARNING THE ART OF BOARDING SCHOOL TEACHING

During my interview with the headmaster, he said that "all faculty received a one-year contract," but he stressed the importance of me staying for at least two years. Although the salary was not great, he assured me that the experience of teaching at the school would be excellent preparation for any other career I might pursue.

I was just happy that he offered me the position and was not thinking about the future. However, during the summer, I had become engaged to Gale, so I wondered how she would like living on campus in a boys' dormitory. As a bachelor living in North Crossley, I spent most of my time with students. In the morning, I got up in time for breakfast in West Hall dining room and checked each room to make sure the boys were ready for breakfast.

One guy from Boston would make up his bed and hide in his closet, so I would think he was on his way, but I got wise to his trick. I sat at the bachelors' table most mornings, but occasionally we had to speak to rowdy students. My first class was at 8 a.m., and I was either teaching or in conferences with students until lunch, where I sat at my assigned table. I had one or two classes in the early afternoon, and then it was time for football practice. We were free to sit wherever we wanted at dinner, but I generally sat with the other bachelors. Free meals were a major part of our remuneration, although we could eat elsewhere if we wanted to.

After dinner, there were intra-dorm softball games, and faculty was expected to attend and supervise. One evening, a fight started between Steve Zabel, on my floor, and Jeff May, on the other team. Jeff landed two punches before we stopped the fight, but his right hand was cut badly, and I had to take him to Franklin County Hospital in Greenfield. The fight occurred near the end of the spring term, so Jeff's hand was in a cast, exempting him from written exams. Most dorm competition was not nearly so exciting.

During the evenings, both faculty and students were busy studying and preparing for the next day's classes. Teachers had duties and responsibilities in the dorm office, but each floor master was ultimately responsible for maintaining quiet and proper behavior during study hours. The floor masters allowed some students to go to the library to study or do research, but a proctor was there, along with the librarian to maintain order.

Study hall was over at 10:15 p.m., and lights went out was at 10:30. The student floor leader checked each room and gave the teacher or floor master the check-slip, certifying that all students were in their rooms for the night. Even if I was not on dorm duty, I had to check student behavior occasionally, wherever I was in the dorm.

One evening, when I was leaving the apartment of a colleague on another floor, I had to reprimand a student for using profanity as he was entering the corridor. On another occasion, I stopped some students from dumping a trash can, full of snow, into another student's room. For such reported infractions, students received demerits. Of course, different teachers reacted differently to such incidents. My approach was to always remind the students about improper behavior and violations, but I gave warnings for first-time offenses.

DEVELOPING NEW COURSES

From my first day in class, I began to realize just how limited my knowledge was. I had some very sharp kids in class, and they occasionally asked difficult questions that I couldn't answer. There was usually a student who relished stumping the teacher in every class, but I told my students that I was young and was learning, like them, and was sure that some of them were smarter than me. I promised to be prepared for every class and would expect them to be also. I told them they could expect a quiz at least once a week after one boy informed me that Marvin Myers began each class with a quiz.

My colleagues in the department were committed to emphasizing critical thinking, problem solving and oral presentations. All 3 presumed a knowledge of the facts in the readings. I tried to encourage students to offer opinions on the readings, films and lectures, and I required short oral presentations, which were difficult for some students (especially foreign students with heavy accents).

I explained my rules and expectations regarding attendance, tardiness, proper dress and respect for others. The school dress code required a dress shirt and tie, and no hats in class, and I enforced this code. Of course, some students tested me by wearing a hat in class or putting their heads down on the desk during class, or taking off their tie in class, or their shoes, or propping their foot up on another chair. One guy asked why I prohibited hats in class, when other teachers allowed it. I answered that I was responsible for my *own* classes, and he must respect my rules.

One day, a boy yawned while I was explaining something, and I lost it. I threw a piece of chalk at him, which shattered on his desk. I told him to "get out" and go to the dean's office. I felt bad about my emotional reaction, but later that day, one of his classmates told me, "I'm glad you did that, because that kid is rude in other classes and gets away with it." In the Class of 1965 Yearbook, students described me as, "takes little gas," for my temper.

The history department endorsed my new course on Sub-Saharan Africa, but only on the condition that I include a large unit on geography, using the two-volume study *TROPICAL AFRICA*, by George H.T. Kimble. We focused on the topography, rivers and lakes, mountain ranges, deserts, grasslands, forest and natural resources. Lots of films and other audio-visual aids were available from university film libraries, which students enjoyed. My slides from Liberia came in handy at different points in the course. We talked about valuable mineral deposits, like iron, bauxite, manganese, copper, tin, cobalt, zinc and others, and the exploitation of these riches and how the foreign companies enjoyed most of the profits.

In the second semester, we studied the various ethnic groups, languages, and the ancient African kingdoms and city-states. This course was an elective for sophomores, and I generally had a class of 12 to 16 students. The other courses on Africa that I created included African Nationalism, Traditional Religion and Culture in West Africa. Throughout my 36 years at the school, I taught a course on African Affairs during any given time. I was surprised to learn that the founder of the African National Congress in South Africa, Pixley Simi, graduated from Mount Hermon.

In 1989, during my second sabbatical, Nelson Mandela's oldest daughter, who was doing a master's program at the University of Massachusetts, agreed to teach my spring term elective on African Nationalism. I used Mandela's autobiography, *Long Walk to Freedom*, 1994, in my last elective on African Nationalism.

There were no separate courses on African American history or literature in 1965 at Mount Hermon or Northfield schools. None of the faculty felt confident enough to offer such courses. As the number of Black students increased, two members of the U.S. Lecture Course agreed to offer a course on the Negro in American History. I taught two sections for a year, but then I introduced a full-year course on African American History that satisfied the department requirement for U. S. History.

It was a popular course, drawing both white and Black students. I used John Hope Franklin's *From Slavery to Freedom* as the main text, supplemented by more specialized works like *Black Power*, by Charles Hamilton and Stokely Carmichael, *Up from Slavery*, by Booker T. Washington, *The Souls of Black Folk*, by W.E.B. Dubois and an anthology of African American literature.

The course I taught was popular from 1968 to1973, during the height of Black student activism on both campuses. At that time, I agreed to teach two sections of American National Government and Civil Liberties, a full-year elective, satisfying the U. S. History requirement. Once again, I had to do considerable summer reading to prepare for this demanding course. I continued to offer my electives on African History and culture.

In the 1990s, I introduced a course on "Minorities in America" as a one-term elective, dealing with Blacks, Latinos and American Indians. Current Issues became a popular elective, and I taught two sections dealing with topics like "The Israeli/Palestinian Conflict," "The Nicaraguan Revolution," "The Right to Privacy in America" and similar important issues. Obviously, I had to do a lot of reading to prepare for these electives, which took up much of my time during school breaks.

All History department teachers were competing for the same pool of students, which became a source of conflict at times. In my last few years, I returned to teaching American History and served as the coordinator of the several sections.

RETURNING TO GRADUATE STUDIES
AND GROWING OUR FAMILY

In my second year, I decided to pursue a master's degree in U.S. History at the University of Massachusetts in nearby Amherst. There was no requirement by the administration that faculty have advanced degrees. In fact, some of the senior master teachers only had B.A. degrees. But when I discovered that the school would pay my tuition and other expenses as long as I was a full-time teacher, I enrolled in the M.A. program.

I changed my coaching assignment from JV football to C squad football, which didn't practice on Wednesday, making it possible for me to take courses at the university. By doing course work through the summer, I was able to complete the requirements and was awarded the degree of Master of Arts in History in October 1967.

Right after graduation in June 1967, Gale and I drove up to Montreal to spend a day at *Expo 67*. It was an exhausting trip, and I had to be back the next day to start summer school at the university. We had no children at that time, and we were both busy with our jobs and school responsibilities. I often wonder how I was able to finish that degree. Five years later, I completed my Doctor of Education degree at the University of Massachusetts.

We lived in my 3rd N. Crossley apartment for a year before moving to the first floor S. Crossley apartment. In May 1966, Gale was 6 months pregnant with twins, but they were born too early and survived two days in an incubator—a boy and a girl, together weighing not quite 4 pounds. Obviously, this was an extremely difficult time, especially for Gale, who had no family nearby.

The school community took us in their warm embrace and arranged for the burial of our twins in the small cemetery near the library in center Gill. Faculty wives prepared dinners and offered words of comfort and love. I can never forget how wonderful the Mount Hermon community was to us during such a difficult time. Other faculty wives who had lost children talked to us about how they dealt with their loss and assured us that time would heal our pain.

Our first son, Channing, was born on September 14, 1969. At that time, we had just moved into Hayden Hall in the center of the campus. We had the second-floor apartment above the lobby and dorm entrance. Gale made beautiful draperies for the large windows that looked out over the first-floor roof and Crossley field. The rooms were large, but the bathroom adjacent to the kitchen, was small.

After Channing was born, Gale began experiencing severe pain from her gallbladder and underwent surgery to remove it. Her mother came up from Georgia to help care for Channing, and when she left, there were other faculty wives who were also helpful in caring for our son.

It was Christmas vacation. The dorm was empty, the temperatures were in the teens and twenties and the heating system had problems. Fortunately, the school plumber, who lived in Bernardston, spent the night in Hayden, keeping the heat flowing to our apartment.

Channing was a beautiful baby boy, and when Gale took him out to the games, the other wives and girls came to get a look at the first African American born in the community. He seemed to be developing normally, but he was quite hyperactive. One night, after we moved into the center faculty apartment in Wallace Hall, Channing had a seizure while sleeping, which lasted more than 30 minutes.

We took him to the hospital, where he was treated and given anti-seizure medicine. He continued to have seizures (but mild ones), and we went to Children's Hospital in Boston, where doctors suggested some form of chemical abnormality in the brain. Yet various physicians were unwilling to give us a conclusive diagnosis. There were suggestions that he might be autistic, based on his behavior.

Even after our son's seizures stopped, his hyperactivity continued. He liked to engage in repetitive motions, like rocking back and forth in his crib, opening and shutting doors and cabinets, and turning lights on and off. His speech development was not normal, and he liked to run away. When we tried to enroll him in the campus nursery school, his behavior was too much of a problem. We found a nursery school for handicapped and retarded children at Deerfield Academy that accepted him. He had some problems getting along with the other kids, like sharing toys, but we all saw some improvement.

Programs like *Sesame Street* seemed to soothe Channing, who loved music. Unlike other boys his age, he showed little interest in what I was doing around the house and outside. He preferred to runoff into the woods or across the fields. When he reached school age, we enrolled Channing in Gill Elementary school as a special student, and he spent lots of time in their resource room with a teaching aide. A local lady, hired by the school system, drove him to and from school.

On May 17, 1973, our second son, Sterling was born. I took Channing with me to the hospital to see Gale and the baby. She and Baby Sterling were doing fine and would be released the next day. On the way home, I stopped at McDonalds for a hamburger and fries (Channing loved them) when a car behind us hit my bumper rather hard.

When I got out to check on possible damage, Channing was trying to climb out of his car seat and turn the steering wheel. When I asked for the other driver's license and insurance information, he was rude and insisted I was worried for nothing, so I quit the argument and hurried back to tend to Channing, who required constant watching while awake. Although we were worried about how he would react to his baby brother, he seemed to be typically curious and considerate most of the time.

MOVING TO BEVERIDGE HOUSE ON "SENILITY HILL"

After 9 years, living in 3 different dorms, we had enough seniority to move to a house on campus. The Donovans were retiring and moving to a house they owned in Amherst. The dean said we could have that house, and we accepted it. Tommy invited me to come up and start my garden in his spot, and I did. He had a garden next to his lawn about 70 x 2 feet, but he encouraged me to expand it. When they moved out in June, I began painting some of the rooms during evenings. The plant and property department provided the paint, rollers, brushes and drop cloths, and we did the painting. We moved in during July. The house, built in 1963, was one mile from the Highway Route 10. It was so quiet that first night that I had a hard time sleeping.

Beveridge House was one of 3 houses built on the top of the campus, just past Ford Cottage, the headmaster's house. The first occupants were senior faculty, hence the name "Senility Hill." Each house had 3 bedrooms, living room and dining room-combined, kitchen, and one and a half bathrooms. There was a full basement and two-car garage and a fireplace. They were spaced at a reasonable distance from each other.

Beveridge House was mainly red brick, except for the garage. The others were painted clapboard houses. We had a full-size kitchen, and the others had a nice screened-in porch. Up to that point we had no utility bills, but at the new house, we had to pay for our electricity and heating. That was the year the oil cartel (OPEC) began cutting production and raising the price of heating oil and other fuels. We set our thermostat at 65 degrees, which seemed to keep the monthly bill down. It was great having a fireplace, and we spent hours enjoying its warmth.

During that time, I decided to pursue another degree at U Mass. The School of Education had a great Doctor of Education program, designed for people already well into their professions. Other faculty members who were taking courses there encouraged me to do so. I had to get an advisor, form a committee and plot out the courses I wanted to take that would lead to a doctorate degree. Because Northfield Mount Hermon was still paying the bill for full-time faculty graduate work, I enrolled.

The Ed.D. program required two years in residence with full-time course work, a dissertation, approved by a committee of 3 advisors and a comprehensive exam by my committee. My original advisor moved out of the area, so I had to find another advisor who would agree to my proposal. Fortunately, I got Professors Bill Kornegay, George Urch, and Sidney Kaplan to guide my research and ultimately approve my dissertation.

My course work focused on the foundations of American Education, African American Education, and African Education and Culture. The title of my dissertation was *MASSACHUSETTS BLACKS AND THE QUEST FOR EDUCATION, 1638 TO 1860.*

It took me 4 years to complete the Ed.D. program. There were several other Hampton graduates studying at the School of Education, including a famous student who purchased a home nearby with his wife.

BLACK STUDENT ACTIVISM BRINGS ON CHANGE

When I arrived on campus in September 1964, there were about 12 Black students—only 4 or 5 in the senior class. I had only a few of these

boys in my 4 U.S. History classes. Although the school did not ask me to
be an advisor to Black students, I gradually got to know a few of them.

By 1967, some of these guys began talking about getting together for a
dinner to become more acquainted and discuss their feelings about being
in a predominantly white environment, but not much came of it. However,
in the next year, with an increase in their numbers and urban uprising
taking place across the country, about 12 students began meeting to talk
about the need for changes in the curriculum, and an increase in the
number of Black students and faculty.

The assassination of Dr. Martin L. King, Jr. served as the catalyst for
the founding of the Afro-Am Society. From its inception, the members of
this group were divided over the question of whether it should be an all-
Black society or open to any interested students. The 4 or 5 students who
seemed to be the most influential among the Black students on campus
argued for an all-Black organization, with its meetings closed to other
students.

Tony Garcia, Cornell Hills, Rodney Antrum, Ken Witherspoon and
David Robinson were clearly the most outspoken members of Afro-Am
and held sway over the group. At one of their organizational meetings, I
congratulated the group for its commitment to the cause of diversity on
campus, but I expressed my opposition to it being a closed, all-Black
group. I spoke about the ideals and goals of the larger civil rights
movement, to abolish segregation in any form.

Unfortunately, my advice was not appreciated at that time. Tony
Garcia, the most militant spokesperson, seized that opportunity to
challenge my position. I urged the members to think seriously about taking
a position that would clearly lead to confrontation with white students and
faculty, some of whom were sympathetic to the society's overall goals.

After the meeting Tony, Cornell and David came to my apartment,
trying to smooth over the obvious disagreement with me, but I was not
willing to accept a policy of Black separatism. They went to Chaplain
Glen Jones for advice. I continued to attend the group meetings and
offered whatever help I could as the discussions of membership dragged
on.

It was obvious that I had misjudged the depth of frustration and sense
of alienation that some Black students felt during that period in our
history. These young men had witnessed the television coverage of the
assassinations of Malcolm X, then Dr. King and the resulting riots in cities
that some called home. Many felt guilty, being there in New England,
while the cities burned, and police and the National Guard controlled the
streets.

An all-campus meeting in Camp Hall auditorium convened to discuss racial tensions on campus stemming from the Afro-Am Society activities. Tony Garcia stood and expressed in very candid, frank and angry terms his feelings about the treatment of Black students by racist police in his city. He clearly and intentionally captured the moment, and the audience was quiet until the Reverend took to the podium and asked that we not lose sight of truth.

In the dorms, racial tensions reached a peak, as some white students challenged the legitimacy of the Afro-Am Society and its separatist policy. Black and white students got into heated arguments about perceived slights and racist comments. There were a number of Black students who did not agree with the Afro-Am's separatist policy, and there were arguments and fights within the group.

One night in South Crossley, an interracial group wanted to stay up beyond dorm closing to continue their discussion, so I urged the house master to let them stay up and continue talking. The discussion was helpful, with a few white students challenging the Black students' positions. The topics discussed included Black students' big Afro hair style, issues about open windows during the winter, and perceived insensitive comments in classes or in the dining hall, where whites wondered about the table with all Blacks. I tried to stay out of the discussion and just let them talk until they were tired. It broke up shortly after 1:30 a.m.

There was a Chinese student, *Noel Chan, who had attended most of the Afro-Am meetings, which raised the question about membership policy. Joel was close with some of the "brothers," and as a result, drew criticism and scorn from unidentified whites in Crossley, who posted a note over his door that read, "Noel Chigger lives here." That note set off a fury, as accusations flew over the source of the note.

Noel was in one of my classes, and he was an academically strong student who appeared to be in rebellion against the religious conservatism of his father back in his homeland. He was more loyal to Afro-Am than most of the other members, and his presence allowed some to argue that the society was open to all.

The chairman of Readers Digest Board and an alumnus donated funds to the school, some of which were to be used to further the school's diversity efforts. The school treasurer purchased refrigerators and furniture for the two rooms designated as meeting rooms for the Afro -Am groups on Mount Hermon and Northfield campuses.

After discussions about the proper use of the fund, there was resistance to yield control to students in the group. So I drew up a proposal for the Society and its *raison d'etre*—its justification to exist and a set of principles governing its relationship with the school, faculty and its overall objectives. I submitted this to the headmaster and ultimately met with him and a few others to discuss and finalize the proposal. They agreed and offered their support for my leadership with the group.

Both the headmaster and chaplain were glad that my relationship with the Society's leaders had improved, but I assured them that I would not be a rubber stamp for ill thought-out policies and actions by militant students, some of whom had called me an "Uncle Tom." I had spoken with several Black students and their parents about their concerns about "separatism" on campus. Some said, in no uncertain terms, that they didn't send their sons to the school to practice segregation. I was clearly in a difficult position in trying to reconcile these conflicting ideas and aspirations.

I reminded the headmaster that I was not hired to be an advisor to Black students, and I was taking on this responsibility voluntarily, even though I had a full schedule of other obligations. I further added that I expected him to support my leadership decisions instead of giving into demands by militants. I was referring to an incident in which a Black student, Ralph Grant, had left campus without permission for Harvard to demand that they accept him for admission after he had been put on the waiting the list.

Tony Garcia, Cornell Hills and one other student insisted on going to retrieve Ralph, even though he had sent a note explaining where he was and why. When they told me of their plans, I argued against their going, as did Dean Torrey, but Arthur Kiendl, the headmaster, overruled our objections and let them go.

I met with Art later and asked why he undermined my position. He told me frankly, "Jerry, I'm the headmaster, and you'll just have to accept my call." He further said that he wanted these Black kids to realize that he was trying to make up for some of the wrongs done to Blacks. The militants in the Afro-Am understood this leverage they had, playing on white guilt, and used it whenever they could.

There were lots of incidents involving conflicting attitudes between Black and white students and *within* the Black student group itself. During that time, young Blacks were embracing cultural nationalism, best expressed by James Brown's song, *I'm Black and I'm Proud!* There was clearly a competition to see who was the "BLACKEST" and the most committed to the militancy, best expressed by the late Malcolm X's *By Any Means Necessary...* Many grew and groomed large Afros, or "Fros," including "Yours Truly," which was seen by some whites, especially those off campus, as a badge of Black militancy.

Curious white students and local store clerks asked silly questions about "Fros," taken as an insult by some Blacks. When some of the "brothers" began sporting mustaches and goatees, some white faculty objected. At a faculty meeting, this topic was addressed and the consensus was that "sporting facial hair was a cultural practice among Black males." Upon hearing that, a Korean faculty member in the history department stood and asked, "What about the yellow people?" which drew laughter. At these discussions, I felt compelled to urge colleagues to show sensitivity toward minority student concerns, but I warned them against creating a double standard that excused students of color from following the rules and academic standards.

In one of my African American History classes, the topic came up about a white actress wearing a cornrow hairstyle, which led to further discussion. In response to a Black girl's charge that the actress was stealing a part of Black culture (appropriation), a white student countered, stating that she thought Blacks should take the gesture as a compliment.

In another class dealing with slave revolts, one white boy said, "Nat Turner didn't seem heroic, because he let his soldiers do the killing of women and children." The comment drew rebuttals from a couple of brothers who seemed angry enough to turn to fisticuffs.

One white boy wondered aloud why Blacks, who had never been to Africa, were adopting African customs and styles. I tried to allow all these issues to be discussed in a civil manner, respecting the different views. I asked all students to offer their criticisms of the course and my teaching by commenting on a blank sheet, without a name, and I had them put the sheets in a box as they left the classroom.

A few chose to sign their names. One boy said that I was too subjective and offered a one-sided view, showing only the negative side. One other white boy wrote that the rotary club in his Maine town would have me fired for some of my comments on race and American foreign policy. I later shared some of this criticism with the class, which were largely positive. I continued that practice in most of my other classes throughout my time at school.

On a specified Monday in November, all Blacks were expected to boycott work, school and their normal activities and instead focus on their history and struggle for freedom. The Afro-Am Society decided to honor that day by marching from the Mount Hermon campus, across the Connecticut River bridge and through the town of Northfield to the Northfield campus. Once there, they would stay together and read poetry, sing songs and talk about Black unity.

The founders of that day of protest wanted to show how important Blacks were through their absence. Local whites didn't know what to make of this all-Black group of 25 students, marching quietly with dignity along the highway and through Northfield. Local government called the state police and Northfield police to chaperone the march, but nothing untoward happened. The students had made their presence known. Even though I didn't march with them, I participated in their meetings that day.

It is not an exaggeration to say that the new militancy and Black consciousness on those two campuses was intimidating and unsettling to several white faculty members. Some of those young Black brothers were aware of their new-found power and used it to their advantage. They walked to classes or school meetings in groups of 3 or 4 with a baleful stare, as if on a mission. They would often arrive late to class and sit together to enjoy the shrill or strident ambiance they brought to the venue. In the dining hall, if a white student tried to sit at the "Black table," he faced that same cold rejection.

Once, a white faculty colleague asked me if he would be welcome sitting at the Black table. When I asked him *why* he wanted to sit there, he said that it bothered him to see an all-Black table. I told him his was not a good reason. Another colleague told me that he was having problems with two Black students who would not take off their hats in class, claiming it was a cultural thing. I told that teacher, "I don't ask white faculty how to deal with white boys who try wearing hats in class. I simply make them remove their hats."

When some artistic brothers decided to paint a mural on the wall in the Black Student Union room, the building janitor alerted the maintenance department. The brothers tried locking the door to prevent curious white students from checking out the place. So it was an unwanted surprise when Black students opened on the weekend and the beautiful mural had been painted over with white paint. When they told me about it, I called maintenance and they told me they ordered the painter to do it, because the brothers never got approval for the mural in the first place. I felt personally disappointed for not being notified so I could inform the group.

The incident raised the issue of the degree of control the Society had over the room, and whether it was off-limits to white students who were not invited. The room was located in the basement of Cutler Hall, the science building at Mount Hermon, and in the Sanda Countway classroom building on the Northfield campus. This issue continued to be divisive among some Blacks, with white roommates and white friends.

CELEBRATING AFRICAN
AND AFRICAN AMERICAN ARTISTIC ACHIEVEMENT

One of the objectives of the Afro-Am Society was to bring recognition to the positive achievements of people of color in the Americas and elsewhere. One way to achieve that goal was by sponsoring an Arts Festival every spring, featuring performances by students of color and speeches by area college professors and celebrities. In the spring of 1969, when the question of whites being members of the Afro-Am Society on both campuses was a hot issue, a reverend from Boston was invited as the keynote speaker to the festival, held on the Northfield campus.

The sisters in the Northfield Afro-Am group allowed some white students to join their society, which set off an argument between the two societies that was addressed at the festival. CBS News sent a reporter and camera crew to Northfield to cover the event, while the reverend took the opportunity to ask the whites to withdraw from the Northfield society. I had no idea that he was going to say what he did, but it seemed to help settle the issue. Thus, the dancing, singing and musical performances by students commenced, as well as displays of their paintings and other artwork. On the whole, it was an extremely successful event, which gave the society and the school helpful publicity.

Black students continued to sponsor an Arts Festival each spring, but the most interesting event took place in April 1974 at Mount Hermon. There were some sisters from Chicago who took my African Nationalism course and had connections with a popular athlete, agreed to attend the festival. We were not convinced that the athlete would actually come, but he did. He spent about 4 hours on campus participating in some of the activities and meeting and greeting students and faculty.

The Northfield Auditorium was usually the venue for events involving the whole school community. In my first year, the school hosted a performance of the powerful Broadway play, *In White America*, which seemed to reflect the school's commitment to the civil rights struggle taking place. Other memorable events included a well-known Nigerian Bongo drummer, who was a historically Black college and university graduate and co-author of a book. I met him in the green room and he gave me an autographed copy of his book.

A famous musical group gave a great performance in the auditorium, and other noted musicians and poets performed at other times. Over the years, the school continued to bring celebrities to campus to speak at Sunday Chapel or all-school assemblies, like the African National Congress representative who asked for our support in the struggle against Apartheid. One such poet thrilled the audience with verses and encouraged students to follow their dreams.

At our commencement ceremonies, we had several African American speakers who were celebrities, athletes or prominent politicians. Some were also alums or had children/students enrolled at the school or were in my classes. Since it is often the policy of schools to let the senior class vote on the commencement speaker, there was a particular year when they selected Sidney Poitier to deliver the commencement speech in the Northfield Auditorium, which was well received, despite the constant flashing of cameras. His daughter, Pam, was in the senior class.

DEVELOPING A COMPREHENSIVE POLICY OF DIVERSITY

I was committed to the goal of increasing the number of minority students and faculty from my very first year at the school. During my interview in 1964, there was no suggestion that I might be an advisor to students of color. I was hired to teach, coach and be a dorm floor master. That was my full-time job, and any other contributions I chose to make were to be voluntary. However, I got involved in new course development and minority teacher recruitment in 1966, and I continued my efforts through my time at the school.

In 1966, I went to Hampton to help interest students in opportunities for minority teachers in New England independent schools. It was a new experience for me, and I enjoyed the opportunity to travel and to meet interesting young college students. However, I was competing with representatives from major corporations, like Mobil Oil, Honeywell and Gillette, who had solid salary-specific and benefit packages to show the seniors they interviewed. I, on the other hand, could only speak in general terms about the opportunities, the quality of students and the benefits and general salary range at some schools.

I could not make a specific offer on behalf of Mount Hermon or any other school. I was thrilled, however, that one of my interviewees was a young lady from my hometown, but she eventually took a job in an urban center. I returned to New England and submitted my report to the committee at The Chocolate School.

Eventually, our advertisements at historically Black colleges began to meet with success. We hired Hamptonian Sam Luke, an economics major, who taught in the History department for a couple years. Luke was from Antigua and had decided to resume his graduate studies. He was an effective teacher, fulfilling his other responsibilities with dignity, but he felt a little isolated as a bachelor in that environment.

Northfield School hired Bobbie Swain, a young Black biology major from Dickenson, who grew up in Talladega, Alabama. Bobbie taught biology and science courses, and she was a dorm parent. In addition, she helped advise the Black students and got along well with the girls as well as Mount Hermon students after the schools merged—all while doing an excellent job. She became good friends with me and Gale and our boys, and in 1973, she moved on to the Friends School on Long Island.

Reverend Young il Shin, a Korean and his wife, Bora, a concert pianist, joined the Northfield and Mount Hermon faculty in 1968. He was fluent in Korean, Japanese, Chinese and English, and he taught Asian studies, while Mrs. Il Shin taught music and offered piano lessons. Young was a close friend and colleague and had a positive impact on our diversity program as adviser to the growing Asian Students organization. Their children were outstanding students at NMH.

There were also two young African teachers appointed, Chanda Mulenga from Zambia, who taught math, and David Mpongo, who taught government and civil liberties as well as U.S. History. When Chanda got married in his first year, the faculty donated a sizable sum of money to him for his bride price. David was an important figure in the nationalist party, Zimbabwe African National Union and part of ZANU's United Nations delegation. He was working on a master's degree at the University of Massachusetts. Unfortunately, he was killed in a tragic car accident on Route 63 while returning from Amherst. I delivered the eulogy at the memorial service for him in the Mount Hermon Chapel.

Our search for Blacks in the administration also bore fruit with the acquisition of Dr. Carey Bell as associate dean at Mount Hermon and house master in a small boys' dorm. He was finishing his Ed.D. at the University of Massachusetts in Amherst, while his wife was teaching French at nearby Deerfield Academy. After Dr. Bell moved on to a better position, John Gooden, a single Black parent, was appointed dean at the Mount Hermon campus.

In 1975, Raymond Harvey, an Oberlin graduate, was hired as choral director. I was an advisor to him in his first year, but he was not comfortable with the arrangement. He was an excellent director and went on to direct orchestras in several major cities.

Barry Brooks, a Black alumnus of Mount Hermon School, joined our counseling department as a part-time advisor to Black students. His home was in Amherst, and he spent a couple days a week on campus with the students at the Afro-Am room. Jean Moss, also a counselor to Black students, joined soon thereafter. She had 3 children attending Mount Hermon. They were all good students and outstanding athletes. Both Barry and Jean made major contributions to minority students and our diversity program.

In the 1980s, we were looking for a dean of Minority Affairs, or someone capable of putting together and strengthening our program of diversity. By then, I was a National Association of Independent School Board member and served on its Academic Committee. As such, I was involved at the national level with the minority teacher and student recruitment effort.

At one of our meetings, Phillips Andover Academy headmaster Ted Sizer, one of the leading supporters of A Better Chance, proposed a one-week summer conference/workshop of minority teachers in member schools at Phillips Academy to discuss and design a working plan to hire more minority teachers. I attended the conference and was pleased that we made progress.

Since school heads seemed slow to hire minority faculty, we demanded their commitment to take a chance on some of the qualified candidates we presented. Ted Sizer promised to offer a job to one of the teachers at the meeting and to give some credibility to our efforts. He kept his promise and offered a Black Math teacher from a private school in the Bronx a job at Phillips Andover Academy. When Sizer told us about the salary scale at Andover, I realized I would have been earning a lot more there than in my current Northfield Mount Hermon position. Several Mount Hermon teachers had joined the Academy over the years, and I could have pursued that option, but I chose not to.

When I served on the NMH Board of Trustees, I led an effort to develop a specific group of data on our past and present Black student population. Based on my years at the school, I knew the names of the students, but there were some who questioned the ethics of such data. I had sent out a questionnaire to those individuals who I knew. Several returned the completed forms, with helpful information about their reasons for choosing the school, what they liked and disliked about their experience and suggestions about ways to increase the number of Black students. NMH dean of faculty supported my efforts and gave me some time to complete my research.

One well-known celebrity had children at NMH and provided a check for the Black Parents' Association. His suggestion that we look for "minority," as opposed to "Black" teachers implied to me that not enough Blacks were qualified or interested. I didn't consider that effort successful. Our search for a minority dean never quite achieved its objective either.

The school hired a young Black woman with some administrative experience, but not as a dean. They gave her a few roles involving Minority Affairs and Student Activities, and she left after two years. Ralph Bledsoe, a Black alumnus from the 1980s, also applied for the position of minority dean, but the school eventually appointed him to teach Science, coach football and be a floor master in a dorm.

The reason we could not fill the dean's position was a combination of inadequate salary and a refusal to make the position a significant one that would attract a real, qualified person. The attitude of the administration was that any appointee should have other areas of responsibility so that he or she would better fit into the community.

WHY I STAYED AT NMH FOR SO LONG

When I began my first year at Mount Hermon, I had no idea that I would stay long enough to become the senior member of the faculty. My original cash salary, $4,500, was disappointing, but free housing and meals, health insurance and no transportation expenses seemed to make the total remuneration competitive. I was able to buy a new Ford Custom 4-door sedan in 1965 after selling my old worn-out Plymouth.

After speaking with other first-year faculty, I learned that I was making more than some. After all, I had two years of experience in Liberia! I was so busy trying to prove myself a good teacher, dorm parent and coach that I didn't have a lot of time to compare my situation with teaching or administrative positions elsewhere. When I was awarded a National Defense Educational Fellowship to study American Historiography at Clark University in Worcester, Massachusetts, it proved helpful and enjoyable to me.

Besides me, there were two young Black female teachers from Alabama in the group of 50 scholars. We listened to lectures from area professors and spent much time reading and discussing interesting topics. I also had sharpened my tennis skills at Mount Hermon, playing students and some teachers, which helped me form friendships with several older guys at Clark.

Gale and I agreed to wait until she completed her B.A. degree at Albany State before getting married. Once she graduated, I drove down South to see her in my new car. We tied the knot at Gale's house in Columbus, Georgia, in the presence of her family and friends, and my mother and her aunt, who had traveled by train from New Jersey.

We had decided not to have a big wedding, so Gale's college roommate, served as her maid-of-honor, and her brother-in-law was my best man. And while Gale's father promised to give us $1,000, he never did. After spending our wedding night in a motel near Fort Benning Military Base, we traveled back to Mount Hermon, stopping in Williamsburg, Virginia, Washington, D.C. and Scotch Plains.

I received a $300 raise in my letter of contract, mailed to all faculty on February 14th, Valentine's Day. My expenses had increased, beginning with the monthly car payment, the new bedroom suite I purchased in June, and higher health insurance to cover a married couple. I was sure that we would not take all our meals in the dining hall, so we had a small food bill as well.

Since Gale was a very good seamstress, we bought a new Singer sewing machine, and she made all her own clothes. She got a part-time job at the Experiment in International Living, just across the border in Vermont. When the campus audio-visual director died, Gale sought and earned that position.

Her facility was in the basement of Beveridge Hall, my classroom building. She assumed the position at a time when the use of films and other audio-visual aids was increasing for all departments. Her office and projectors and other equipment were adjacent to the 80-seat auditorium where most faculty brought their classes for viewing.

She ordered all the films, slides and recordings from various film libraries, and she was responsible for the set-up when films were shown in Camp Hall or the chapel.

Gale had student assistants who completed their assignments with her. During the summer, she continued working, but on a part-time basis, holding the position until Channing was born. After we moved the Wallace Hall Dorm, she served as a dorm parent. She was popular with the Afro-Am students, and they spent time in our apartment as a home away from home.

After the birth of our second child, Sterling, Gale took an executive secretary position at ICE (Incentive Community Enterprises), an organization that arranged employment for handicapped adults. She commuted to Greenfield and Northampton during that time, and she also worked at the Franklin County Hospice program. Gale's mom came to live with us in 1992, but as her health declined, Gale discontinued her employment to provide care for her mom.

Gale's first year at Mount Hermon was a bit uncomfortable due to the severe winter that year. She was shy and felt awkward around the mothers on campus. After we lost the twins in the spring of 1966, it was especially difficult for her, being distant from her family. Her father refused to loan her the money for a plane ticket during her Christmas visit, so she had to take the bus while 4 months pregnant, from Columbus back to N. J., where I was staying with my family until she returned.

Gale was happy that we had a comfortable living arrangement, and even though our combined earnings were meager, my job was secure, and we didn't have to call on our parents for help. When I described my job to my father's barber shop buddies, one guy commented that I was already in Heaven! Anyway, we decided to stay at Mount Hermon. I continued to get annual raises, and we moved to a larger apartment on first floor of South Crossley.

As I earned my two graduate degrees, I began considering a college teaching position. Several faculty colleagues had moved on to better jobs at other independent schools and colleges. At the university in Amherst, there were many doctoral candidates who were pursuing degrees in school administration and leadership. I began hearing about positions I could attain, so I put out some feelers and made some calls, but in the end, the salary and benefits I earned at Mount Hermon were more attractive, especially considering Gale and the boys.

When I got my Ed. D., I applied to Johnson C. Smith University in Charlotte, Holyoke Community College, Hampton Institute and Morgan State University. However, I would have started as an instructor, or associate professor, and would have had to provide my own housing.

We loved the campus environment, especially with two young boys, and we looked forward to moving into a house for faculty. Whenever I was upset with a school policy or had the urge to move, the headmaster would offer a good raise, better housing, and the chance for my first sabbatical after 7 years.

I was sure that I should and could have been earning a higher salary. On a trip back from a committee meeting in St. Louis, a New York Life representative who I had met earlier told me he was sure I could get a position at his company, considering my experience and degrees. The "grass always looked greener" over there, but I stayed put.

Dr. Bill Campbell, the former chair of the Hampton History department, was the dean of faculty at Holyoke Community College, and he called me and offered me a position as assistant provost for Student Affairs, but I had already signed and submitted my letter of contract. He assured me that he could speak to my school head and release me, but I said "no." I knew Holyoke was having a problem with minority students, specifically Black and Hispanic day students from the city, and I didn't want to get embroiled in that quagmire.

The Southern Association of Independent Schools began a training program for minority headmaster candidates, and my contacts at NAIS named me as a good prospect. The program involved a year of training at a school like Lovett Academy in Atlanta before taking a position as a headmaster at a member school. After a Christian Academy in Thomasville, Georgia, that sought to diversify its faculty contacted me, the school head told me I came highly recommended. He admitted, however that the school and community were "quite conservative," compared to Mount Hermon. I decided not to follow up on the offer.

Gale was supportive of my decision to remain at NMH because she loved the safe rural campus environment for our two boys. Channing, with the help of teachers and psychologists, eventually grew out of some of his bothersome and scary behavior. We enrolled him in the Devereaux School in Rutland, Massachusetts, which was difficult for us, but helpful to him. When he returned home, he was much happier and more responsible. He had found comfort zone and self-esteem through playing tennis.

He completed his high school education at Turner's Fall High, where he excelled in tennis and competed on the JV basketball team. He won several tennis awards and tournaments and was the top player at the high school. In 1987, Channing got his driver's license and began driving out to area malls as his weekend entertainment. He got a full-time job in West Hall and held that job until 1995.

Sterling, who was 4 years younger than Channing, was on track to enter NMH as a freshman in 1987. As a faculty child, he was entitled to a free ride through the 4 years. He could have lived in a dorm, but he chose to be a campus day student. This great benefit was one of the reasons I stayed on until retirement. For both our boys, my uprooting them during their formative years would have more negative than positive consequences.

In my heart, I had come to think of Mount Hermon as "home," the place where I felt the most comfortable. Our colleagues and neighbors were good, caring people, even though the school population had grown.

We loved our house and its location in a quiet part of the campus, as well as our yard, the garden and my wood lot across the road, where I cut firewood, and where Sterling and friends built their tree house. The 3 clay tennis courts at Ford Cottage were just up the road from our house, and we played there in the evenings. Both Channing and Sterling were good tennis players, and there were several courts available at different dorms.

They also had access to Forslund Gymnasium and its weight room, basketball courts and swimming pool. It was almost like living at a resort, especially during the vacations, when most students went home. We also could call on Plant & Property, the maintenance department, when any repairs or service on the house were required. It's hard to put a value on that benefit. During my last few years, I enjoyed running and walking the cross-country trails through the woods, and down to the lower fields near the Connecticut River, and back up on campus through the apple orchard.

The school covered my graduate school tuition and other expenses and awarded me 3 sabbaticals. The first was in 1978, after I had just completed my doctorate, and I took the spring term off to do some writing. In 1989, I used my time to visit presidential homes and museums on the east coast.

I took off an entire year in 1998-99 to study Spanish, learn to play the guitar, and read works by Hispanic writers. In the winter and spring, Gale joined me on a 10-day trip to Mexico, visiting the Mayan ruins and Cancun. In the remaining time, I took a road trip through the Southwestern states, and a two-week trip to South Africa in June-July.

I was thrilled with having the opportunity to visit South Africa. I had been studying and teaching about the people, the climate, the natural resources and the struggle against Apartheid since my first year at Mount Hermon. I had several Black students from Soweto, Alexandra, Germiston, and Cape Town, who described their experiences growing up in a country where the white minority controlled the government and the wealth of the country. Representatives from the African National Congress had spoken to my classes, including James North, the author of *Freedom Rising,* a first-hand look at life under Apartheid, which my students found compelling.

I joined a group of students and teachers from Michigan on a tour that took us to Johannesburg, Pretoria, Swaziland, KwaZulu-Natal, Durban, East London, Cape Town and to several other places. We didn't visit any Black townships for security reasons.

Thabo Mbeki, Nelson Mandela's successor, was being inaugurated as president during our stay in Johannesburg, and many foreign heads of states were there, necessitating a heavy military security presence. I had no role in planning the itinerary, but I tried to see as much of the country as I could.

I took early morning walks to the local towns near the facilities where we spent our overnights. I met both men and women on their way to work, and I greeted them in Swahili, "Habari za Asubuhi," or in Zulu, "Sawubona." The black people who I greeted were all friendly, and while some immediately recognized me as an American, others (including waiters and workers) addressed me as "baas" or boss, embarrassing me.

The Afrikaners I encountered were pleasant, but they spoke of the African population as a monolithic group of "Blacks" when referring to their customs and behavioral characteristics. Occasionally, I heard some whites complain about Affirmative Action policies, which were responsible for the number of Blacks in media and government positions.

Political correctness was just beginning to influence the conversation and discussion on social and political issues, and our students were surprised by some of the comments from whites.

We spent the first two days in Johannesburg and Sandton before traveling by tour bus North to Tshukudu Game Lodge Reserve. We remained two nights there, housed in traditional rondavel huts, equipped with electric power and plumbing. There, we drove and walked through the parks with lions, leopards, elephants, rhinos, hippos, giraffes and other wild animals and reptiles.

The destructive power of elephants was evident from the ruined trees and bushes they fed on and trampled. We learned to never turn our backs on a wild animal, especially the cats and lions, and we understood that we were safe in their environment, as long as we remained up on the big land rovers. Kruger National Park, which encompassed Tshukudu and several other lodges, was near the border of Mozambique. I noticed that while the custodians and managers at these parks were both whites and Blacks, whites were in control of most facilities.

The rest of our journey was to the south, through Malelane Gate, and then Swaziland, spending an overnight in both places. Swaziland is a mountainous country, and the view from Piggs Peak was spectacular. The country shared an eastern border with Mozambique, not far from the capital of Maputo. In Mbabane, Swaziland, we shopped and dined at a mall before being entertained by traditional African dancers at night with an outdoor fire.

Groups of kids approached our bus in Mbabane, begging for money, but our leader discouraged us from being generous, as these kids often used the money to by glue to sniff. Crossing the border back into South Africa, we headed south to Kwa Zuluand, where we stayed one night at a farm that was owned by an English lady, who had arranged for our tour of a Zulu village.

The chief offered us traditional beer in gourds, passed around, and since I was the oldest man in the group, I took the first gulp. It tasted like warm beer—not as good as a cold Bud Light! The women, in their traditional dress, prepared a delicious meal, including the staple mealie pap, which was similar to grits.

The next leg of our journey included an overnight in Umhlanga, enjoying a day on the beach and shopping briefly in Durban, a bustling city with a large Indian population on the Indian Ocean. We flew from Durban to Port Elizabeth, and then we spent a day and night at Plettenberg Bay, a beautiful beach resort, famous for surfing.

Then we were off to Oudtshoorn and the ostrich farm, where we were ate a breakfast of scrambled ostrich eggs, bacon and biscuits. Later, we watched the bungee-jumping (some of our boys included) from the bridge over the Matjies river. Our last stops were at the Cape of Good Hope and Cape Town, where we spent the final 3 days visiting Table Mountain, dining at Victoria and Alfred Waterfront complex and ending with a trip to Robben Island, where Nelson Mandela was imprisoned for 20 years. I only regret not being able to spend more time here, but after 15 days away from home, I was ready to return.

MY LAST YEAR AT NORTHFIELD MOUNT HERMON

One of my sabbatical resolutions was to study Spanish and read many works of fiction and non-fiction about Hispanic and Latino culture. I enrolled in the Adult Spanish course at NMH, taught by a neighbor and fellow teacher. Our class met once a week, and I put forth my best effort, but I really needed to have an immersion experience in Mexico with a family where only Spanish was spoken.

I also bought a guitar and tried to learn to play some simple tunes, but the effort proved to be more difficult than I expected. In my Minorities in America course, I devoted one-third of the curriculum to Hispanics and Latinos, and I discovered the wealth of interesting novels and non-fiction anthologies, which influenced my sabbatical focus.

At the beginning of the 1999-2000 academic year, I was sure that it would be my last year. I had talked it over with Gale and the boys and discussed retirement with a few faculty colleagues. It was my 36th year at NMH, and there had been so many changes in the schedule and faculty responsibilities, many of which I found difficult to accept. I no longer felt the independence and control I once enjoyed at NMH, and I realized that it was time to begin a new chapter of my life experience. Our sons had become adults after having enjoyed the experience of growing up on the campus, but they were prepared for us moving away.

Sterling had graduated from NMH, Emerson College in Boston, and had begun his career in Los Angeles. Channing was living with us and would join us in our move to Chatham, Virginia. After Gale's mother, Lucille, died in 1998 after 6 years living with us on campus, we felt the need to spend more time with family. My mother was living alone in Chatham on the family property, and I was really looking forward to being close during her last years.

We had bought a 4-bedroom doublewide mobile home in 1995 and had been staying there on the property during vacations. As we looked forward to relocating, I knew that we would miss the campus and our friends, and I would miss being around young folk. However, I wouldn't mind not spending my nights and weekends correcting papers, because teaching at an independent school was a 7-day job. The novelty of the experience had been exhausted long ago.

By January 2000, I had determined that I would retire in June. Glenn Vandervleit, my good friend and fellow history teacher, decided to retire as well. We spent considerable time talking it over and convincing ourselves to do it. The headmaster tried to convince us to stay, but we were firm in our resolve. He asked me to give the address at the baccalaureate assembly in the auditorium. Glenn gave the commencement address on Thorndike Field.

After 27 years in Beveridge House, we had accumulated more stuff than we realized or needed. As faculty, were expected to pack up our belongings, clean the house and be out before by the last day of June. We managed to get it done by midnight on the 30th, and spent the night at the Windmill Motel, near the campus entrance. On July 1st, we left for

Chatham; Channing drove the car with Gale, and I drove the F-150, loaded down with items that we did not put on the ABF trailer that we sent a day earlier and was waiting for us in our Chatham driveway.

My brothers Joe and Danny came down to Chatham that weekend to helped us unload the ABF trailer that was parked close enough to our front deck that we could easily move the furniture into the house. That night, Gale and I thanked the Lord for allowing us to make the move safely and to begin a new chapter in our lives in Chatham with Mom, Joe and my cousins, who were just a few doors away.

Sister JoAnn at home, 1974

Channing at Washington Monument, 1992

Me and my sons, Channing and Sterling
after church service, Mr. Hermon

Gale, her father, and our sons, Mt. Hermon, 1982

Me and Gale at our wedding, Columbus, GA, 1965

Photos - Section Four

Me and Gale before Commencement, Mt. Hermon

Me, Bobbie Swain and NMH students, 1972

Gale and baby Channing, Mt. Hermon, 1969

Gale, Rainy, JoAnn, Mom and Dad at home, 1966

Me correcting papers in classroom, Beveridge Hall, NMH, 1988

Me and NMH students resting after a fundraising walk,

Kayla Dibble with Muhammad Ali

Me, Gail and Chung Yo Shin, Cornell Hills

History Department Colleagues: Bob, Young l'l, Glenn, and me

Part Five

KEEPING BUSY, PRODUCTIVE AND HAPPY IN RETIREMENT

Our new home, a doublewide 28 x 60-foot Fleetwood mobile home, was set up behind a stand of Virginia pines, about 150 feet from Irish Road. We were just 3 miles west of the Tight Squeeze Shopping Plaza on U.S. Route 29. The town of Chatham is 3 miles north. It was our first time living so close to the road with constant traffic, yet it was definitely rural, pastoral and quiet.

The lot I had cleared of trees and bramble for the home was near fields and the family cemetery; most of the 118 acres was forest. We had allowed the trees to grow since 1965 and now many are saw timber size. A local white tobacco farmer, Giles, was leasing the fields for our tobacco allotment. I was never pleased with that arrangement, but it helped pay our property fees.

Giles had a deer lookout tower built near the back field, and he had sent his crew to clear the small trees that blocked its view. In the summer, they cut and bailed the hay, and his relatives enjoyed hunting rights on the property, which posed problems for our regular walks through the long paths of the woods.

Having lived on the Mount Hermon campus for nearly 4 decades, the reality of retirement was slow to sink-in. We had used the home on vacations and trips since 1995, but our first night there after the move was special, with the sensation of the new environment, the ordeal of unpacking and the anticipation of furnishing the house.

Gale, the master of details, supervised the process. The home did not come with furniture, other than a refrigerator and an electric range. We had only purchased beds and a few lamps, and Gale was looking forward to shopping for new pieces in Danville. In our haste to be out of our campus house by June 30th, we had left several bulky items behind, as well as plants and garden tools, not to mention the green-house and log cabin I had built. There was only so much room in the ABF trailer and our two vehicles, so we told our campus neighbors to help themselves to the items in our two-car garage.

We had a full cellar in Beveridge House, but in Chatham, we had to rely on the one 12 x16-foot shed that Channing and I built in the previous year. The 84 Lumber truck delivered the materials and we put them together, following the plans. Joe, who built his own house in 1991, was still living at home in Plainfield and driving down, periodically, with materials for his project. He had also supervised our roofing job, as I had not shingled a roof before.

Joe was a great help in several construction projects we undertook, including another shed, sidewalks, a rear deck and roof, and a cement platform for a carport. As for Joe's own house, it was a Jim Walters Shell, constructed by a single contractor in two weeks. He completed the interior work, with the help of local craftsmen, relatives and friends. By working with Joe and his buddy, I learned many construction concepts.

Brother George (Danny) had retired and came down occasionally on his Honda Gold Wing. He took long trips and stopped in Chatham for a few days. The 3 of us had many good times, sitting in Joe's yard reminiscing, sharing jokes or working on some project. After we moved, they often joined us for dinner. Joe reminded me how lucky we were to have a maintenance department to handle all repairs at our previous house; "You are going to find out what it's all about when you move," he often said as we worked on his house.

It wasn't long after we moved that brother Joe's prediction came true. The commode in our master bathroom wasn't flushing properly. My attempts to solve the problem failed, so I complained to the company, and they sent out a plumber who had to cut the sewer pipe under the house and remove a rug cutter, which was lodged inside and blocking the flow to the septic tank.

There were a few other problems with leaking pipes in both bathrooms, requiring repairmen from the company to come out on separate occasions. Actually, we were lucky that these were the only serious problems we had. Channing and I had plenty work, which involved landscaping the yard, planting grass, trimming trees and mowing.

We also took over the job of maintaining the cemetery. We began walking the perimeters of the property, looking for old, barbed-wire fences, posts and metal markers. I carried Daddy's old double barrel shotgun, as he did when walking through the woods. At times, we were almost a half mile from the house, so Gale bought a set of two-way radios, allowing us to communicate from a distance.

We seldom saw anyone during these treks, but we observed spent shotgun shells and the old lookout towers where hunters had perched. We found two old logging roads, running the length of the property, that were blocked by trees, brambles and bushes, which we cleared away, allowing me to drive my full-size Ford F-150 down to the end and turn around.

We also discovered 3 tobacco curing-barn stone foundations and the remnants of an old log cabin, with its stone chimney still standing. Although trees covered most of the property, the furrows in the ground evidenced where crops use to grow. We saw deer, wild turkeys quail, and occasionally a black snake.

The lower portion of the property, which we referred to as the "low grounds," were about 100 feet below the houses and the road. The creek flowed through that part from the old spring, the source of water for the families over the years. Our cousin, Acie Junior, set up a pump in the spring to provide water for his trailer in 1976. Daddy and Momma got their water from that same source.

Joe had his own well dug— 300 feet down, and we did the same. During the heavy rains, the creek overflowed its banks and washed up good sand, which we collected for use in building projects. I found many rocks and stones of varying sizes and shapes that I used as borders for gardens and walls, and I spent many hours finding and collecting them and carting them back to central piles. During those forays, I felt a sense of security and comfort, realizing that the property belonged to our family, while thinking of all the projects I wanted to undertake.

After my 62nd birthday on July 9th, 2000, I signed up for Social Security. My first check did not arrive until September, so we had relied on my pension and our savings during the interim. We had paid for the house in full, so we didn't have a mortgage. Our only major bills were for electricity and health insurance. We continued our existing Blue Cross plan, but in retirement, we had to pay the premium, which was gradually increasing. Gale and I enjoyed good health during that period, as our monthly premium took up most of my Social Security check. The Cobra plan ended upon my 65th birthday, and we both enrolled in separate Medigap plans.

In some ways, it felt like we were on an extended vacation, since we usually spent our school breaks in Chatham. Not having to get up early for class or the job—was a relief! No more correcting papers and tests, preparing lesson plans, or reports, and no more committee meetings and school assemblies to attend, or parent conferences! It was the first time in 40 years that I was not under pressure to study or prepare as a student or a teacher.

However, I sometimes awoke from a dream about classes or school activities and realized that I was not there anymore—just dreaming. Yet I still felt the need to keep up with the literature in my discipline and the subjects I taught. I continued buying books, which lined the walls of a few rooms. I left some bookcases at Mount Hermon, so I built some new ones to accommodate my expanding library, which usually provoked the question about how many I had actually read.

One of the joys of living on the family property was being close to Mom. She was doing well for her age, and she content living alone since

Dad's passing. She occasionally suffered sharp nerve pain—neuralgia, and she had cataract surgery in one eye. Mom loved working crossword puzzles, and especially Jumbles and other word games in the newspaper.

She loved the game shows on television, especially *Wheel of Fortune* and *Jeopardy*. We all knew that *you don't call Mom* when *Jeopardy* was on! She watched all the news programs and kept up with national and world events. When she and Dad moved there in 1976, we bought them a subscription for the *Danville Register*, but Mom eventually implored us to discontinue the delivery.

When Joe came down to work on his house, we all spent time with Mom in the evenings, often sitting outside, where it was cooler. She had spent her entire adult life caring for others. While raising her own children, she assumed care of Aunt Jenny during her last years when I was away at college. I know it must have been difficult for Mom. After Dad died in 1983, she was alone for the first time. We all worried about her being so far away from the family in New Jersey and Massachusetts, so we visited as often as possible. Cousin Acie and his wife Mable and children were next door and were helpful.

Mom enjoyed all the simple things, like walking out to the fields to pick a bunch of cress greens for dinner or going down to the spring for a nice cold dipper of water or a cup of Nescafe coffee any time of the day. She never learned to drive, though I tried to teach her after I got my driver's license, but Dad discouraged her, and she lost interest. She rode with Mable or friendly neighbors who drove her to town for shopping or appointments.

After Dad's passing, she went with us to Gale's home in Columbus, Georgia, for Christmas twice and really enjoyed herself and spending time with Gale's mother, who had her own car. She was also happy when Joe began preparing the site for his new house, which he was determined to build on the same lot where two chimneys from the old homestead burned down in 1981. He had a local contractor knock down and remove them.

Mom accompanied Joe to Salem to see the Jim Walters' Shell Homes, and he selected and built one on our lot next to Mom. She was helpful throughout the whole process of completing the house, and meeting and paying the craftsmen, who finished jobs during Joe's absence. She was also the contact person for us when our home was delivered and set up on our lot. We couldn't have done it without her. Even though she could have used her newfound independence after Dad died to travel or do things she always wanted to, she was there for us—helping us realize our dreams.

In August 1995 when I purchased our home, I proposed paying half down and the remainder upon delivery and set-up, but the manager of the company was apprehensive about this arrangement, saying, " What if after we deliver the home, you, for some reason, have an accident and can't pay the balance?" I assured him that we would pay the balance.

However, as things turned out, on our trip back to Chatham to complete the deal, we had an accident on I-64, near Waynesboro. Gale, who was driving, fell asleep, causing the accident. Fortunately, we just ran off the road and didn't collide with any car or object, but we had to be towed to Chatham. It was a sobering and humbling experience. The car was still road-worthy after a new rear wheel and tire, but after that event, Gale was afraid of driving on the long trips.

Six months into retirement, I felt the need to get a part-time job. I had been working or studying since I was a teenager, so it felt strange not having a job. I had plenty of work to do on the property, but I needed to find some way to connect with the surrounding community, and it wouldn't hurt to earn extra money.

I didn't want a teaching position or any job in a school system, so I applied at Lowe's home improvement store and Walmart, but neither called med. Eventually, I answered an ad in the paper for a security job and accepted a job with Burns Security as an unarmed security guard in Blairs, about 6 miles from home.

Etoys had two large warehouses there, with 3 shifts during the Christmas season. I worked there through December 2000 before Burns transferred me to Columbia Forest Products in Chatham, a 3-mile commute. Unlike at Etoys, the Chatham job required only one guard on duty per shift. I worked the 8 p.m. to 8 a.m. shift on the weekends. As the new guy, I filled in for others once I learned the routine. Security was responsible for controlling the traffic into and out of the plant.

Columbia Forest manufactured hardwood plywood for interior use. There was a steady stream of inbound trucks with appointments for delivery, and others came and went, picking up loads from the shipping department. The hardest aspect of the job was staying awake in the early morning hours when there were no trucks arriving. We also had to do walking patrols through the plant and around the perimeter, which I didn't mind, as it broke the monotony of sitting in the guard house. Joe often teased me about falling asleep with slippers on, holding a donut, which a raccoon took away. Actually, I easily adapted to the overnight shift and came to prefer it to first or second.

Working as a security guard was a new experience where my years of professional education were not generally applicable. It was the first job I had applied for since beginning my teaching career. I quickly adapted to the military-type courtesy required in addressing visitors, client staff and employees with a smiling, "Yes sir" or "Yes ma'am." I learned the routine and the process of recording and logging in the trucks, contractors and visitors.

What I didn't particularly like was answering the phone and transferring calls and messages for employees. There was the occasional spouse of an employee who insisted on speaking with an employee who could not or would not answer the radio or phone. I didn't like having to walk up to the plant in rain or snow to unlock a door, which was sometimes irritating. There were times when truck drivers, waiting to unload and reload their trucks, would come into the guardhouse to vent their frustrations while pressuring me to check on the status of their order.

I naturally sympathized with them, since I understood the conditions that they faced on the road. But the forklift drivers who unloaded and reloaded trucks would sometimes get angry when security called to check on a particular shipping order.

Whenever there was an emergency situation in the factory, such as a fire or an injured employee, security communicated with first responders in Chatham. We were prepared for bomb threats, but none occurred during my time there. As for my fellow officers, most were competent, friendly, and easy to work with.

However, after I began working at Columbia Forest Products, I often felt put upon by my supervisors. One fellow who worked the midnight to 8 a.m. shift habitually arrived late. When I questioned him, his excuse was his long commute or oversleeping or car trouble. He never arrived early, allowing me to leave early from my 4 p.m. to midnight shift.

He told me that he had to regularly wait for the first shift officer, the site supervisor, who also arrived late. I found what he said to be true when I had to do the overnight shift. I complained to him about how unfair the practice was and how it was against company regulations. After he had been late several times, he paid me out of his pocket for the inconvenience he had caused.

On one occasion, the male friend of my fellow female officer got into a physical altercation with his friend on the plant property as I was arriving to begin my Sunday 8 p.m. shift. One guy hit the other with a metal arm of a power pressure washer that he had in his truck. After my partner and I stopped the fight, I called the sheriff and the rescue squad which took the injured man to the hospital.

The deputy who questioned me as a witness and told me I would likely have to be in court when the case came up, as the injured guy pressed charges against his friend (whose truck he was borrowing). On the day of the trial and after my partner and I arrived at the courthouse, the charges were dropped, and the case was dismissed.

I did the best I could to follow the rules, take the training courses and avoid problems, and I was promoted to sergeant and weekend shift supervisor. Although, I received awards and plaques for my performance and management encouraged me to pursue higher positions, I was content with my part-time work, the short commute, and the opportunity I had to read and do some personal writing during the quiet overnight hours.

During my 16-year tenure, there were 4 different security companies that held the contract and paid our wages and benefits. I was hired by Burns Security, which later merged with Securitas, an international corporation. Columbia Forest Products kept the same officers on through 4 different security companies. By December 2016, I decided to retire—after a new company was awarded the contract.

During my time at Columbia Forest, I suffered the loss of my mom, in 2003, Gale, in 2013, George Dan, in 2014, and Joe, in 2015. Mom was 90 and had suffered kidney failure. She lived alone in her trailer until 2 months before passing on, at Gretna Health Center. The entire family gathered in town for her funeral service. She was laid to rest next to Dad in the family cemetery. Joe and I and our other siblings had to carry on without our beloved mother.

GETTING INVOLVED IN COMMUNITY AFFAIRS

I began expressing my opinion on local issues through letters to the editor of the *Danville Register & Bee*, the local newspaper, to which we had a subscription to since Mom and Dad moved to Chatham. After we moved south in July 2000, I realized just how conservative many of the county residents were. Like everyone, we were shocked and stunned by the 9/11 tragedy. We watched those planes crash into the World Trade Center Towers and tried to understand how this could happen.

We learned later that a NMH faculty member who left the school for a job in California was on the second plane. He was a young IT specialist, and before we moved, had come to our house to purchase some of the items we were selling.

After the Bush/Cheney administration began the wars in Afghanistan and Iraq, I felt that the march to war was taking place too quickly. I opposed the invasion of Iraq, because Saddam Hussein was not responsible for the 9/11 terrorist attack, and the country was already under a no-fly zone.

As local readers began expressing their support for the U.S. invasion of Iraq, I wrote my first "letter to the editor," entitled, "Let's Think This Through," questioning proposed military policy. I expressed my opposition to the Confederate Flag, flying on public property, which drew a response from the local chapter of the Sons of Confederate Veterans and others of similar ilk.

One lady from Ringgold who took issue with most of my letters called me a "mis-educated northern liberal." Yet I got phone calls from several people in Chatham and Danville, complimenting me for expressing my views. One such supporter, a local minister and member of the county Democratic Committee, invited me to join the committee, which was then chaired by an African American woman.

As a new member of the committee, I was disappointed that more young people were not members or actively involved. I wrote letters to the editor, supporting the Democratic Party principles and policies and highlighting the new voter-restriction laws passed by many Republican-controlled state governments. To encourage more youth participation, I suggested an essay writing contest for local high school students, focused on what the Democratic presidents had done for the American people.

The chair, a few other committee members and I drafted an essay question and offered a $200 prize for the winner. The Pittsylvania County Democratic Committee (PCDC) approved the proposal, and I contributed $200 to cover the prize expense. However, despite our attempts to get several students to participate, only one applicant, a white female student from Tunstall High School, submitted an essay.

It was well-written, focused on the question and won the prize. At the annual PCDC banquet at the C&Es restaurant in Gretna, I presented the prize to the winner.

I became a precinct captain for the Climax Voting District (where I to vote), which is 14 miles roundtrip from my house on Irish Road. Residents on the north side of the road are assigned to that district, which is very rural and had few African Americans, even though the polling officials at the Ruritan Club in Climax were primarily Blacks.

I began making calls to eligible voters, encouraging them to register and vote, while answering any questions they had about the process. I took the training to qualify for helping those eligible to complete the registration form, but I had a difficult time finding a public place to set up a registration table. Most businesses were reluctant to allow a registration table out front on the sidewalk.

Pittsylvania County is very rural and conservative, except for the city of Danville, so it's been difficult to elect Democrats to state and federal offices from the area. As a student and teacher of African American history, I had always admired the NAACP and the great work of its legal defense team, once headed up by the great Thurgood Marshall, the first African American associate justice of the United States Supreme Court.

I joined the Pittsylvania County Branch of the NAACP and chaired its committee on Press and Publicity. Using my letters to the editor, I promoted the work of the branch and invited local media to cover events of the various branch committees. Yet again I was disappointed by the absence of young adult branch members. I joined the Education Committee and helped with the annual scholarship program and presented awards at local high schools.

I became a tutor in the joint tutorial program with the Cherrystone Baptist Church, the NAACP and Chatham Elementary School. I found the weekly sessions with young pupils particularly challenging and rewarding. In 2019, I was the winner of the NAACP Clyde Banks Community Service Award for my work with the local branch and area groups promoting equal justice.

I have always loved reading, especially biographies of people who have helped make a positive difference. The walls of my living and family rooms are lined with the books I have read and hope to read. Occasionally, some visitor will comment about these books and ask me, "Have you read all these books?" I always answer, "Most of them," while realizing that I probably don't remember much of what they contain.

When I learned about the "Brown Bag Book Review" series at the Chatham Public Library, I began attending the lunch-hour presentations and gave reviews of new books I read. The first one was *The Firebrand and the First Lady*, by Patricia Bell-Scott, followed by *Barracoon*, by Zora Neale Hurston, and George Yancy's *On Race: 34 Conversations in a Time of Crisis*, which explored the concept of "white privilege."

My last book review was on David Blight's Pulitzer Prize-winning biography *Frederick Douglass; Prophet of Freedom*, 2018. Attending these reviews, in which participants were mainly white, is the equivalent of taking a graduate school course in the humanities without the essays and exams. As I write these words, I'm thinking of what my next book review will be!

Our Civil Rights is an annual spring/summer discussion series, sponsored by the Pittsylvania County Public Library, in partnership with a few local churches and other groups. These monthly gatherings are open to the public and feature films and lively discussions, led by a local college professor. I have attended each meeting and participated enthusiastically.

Pittsylvania Together, one of the sponsors, is another group I participate in and where I give presentations on the topics of Racism and Civil Rights. I have met and gained several new friends through my participation in these various community groups.

During Gale's long illness, I did not have time to get involved in such groups, but since her passing, the relationships I have formed have been a great comfort to me.

Me and Gale at Amistad Schooner Construction site
Mystic CT, 1998

The Red Rock of Sedona, AZ

Kuku Klan El Castillo Pyramid
at Chichen Itza, Yucatan, Mexico

Me on the steps of the Observatory
at Chichen Itza, 1999

Photos - Section Five

Kwazulu dancers with rondeval huts
made of sticks and straws

Me at Robben Island Prison
after visiting Nelson Mandela's cell

Artifacts store, Tshukudu Game Lodge, South Africa

Mliliwini, Swaziland
Queen Mother's Home

Gale and sisters,
Diane and Rosiland

Family gathering at George Davis funeral, 1983

Photos - Section Five

Sisters Rainy and JoAnn

Doug Jones, Hampton graduate and a life-long friend

McCall P. Skeeter, Hampton graduate and a life-long friend

Part Six

CONCLUSION

Now that I have chronicled the events of my journey so far, I realize just how many specific experiences I failed to delve into. But that's probably true for most autobiographies. Some things are best left in the past. I will say that I regret having waited so late in life to pen these words, when my fading memory has made it difficult to spell out the imagery of some events and occasions. What I regret most is not spending more time talking with my parents and other relatives—and specifically about our family genealogy and what they remembered about their formative years. Because my career pursuits kept me distant from home for a good many years, I missed the opportunity to ask the questions and record the memories they could share.

I suppose it's natural to speculate on how different my life would have been had I not gone away to college, but rather enlisted in the military or taken a full-time job after high school. But at 17 and 18 I was anxious to get away—not so much from family, but from a community that was anything but progressive.

I had narrowly escaped getting caught up in some of the dangerous habits and activities that influenced some of my peers and limited their potential. I credit my neighbor and mentor, Mrs. Grobes, and her daughter for inspiring me to reach out and embrace new experiences and discover new environments.

As a caddy for Mrs. Grobes daughter, I traveled to golf tournaments in Philadelphia, Cleveland and Washington D.C. as a 14-15-year-old, meeting important and interesting people who all encouraged me to "Stay in school" and "Be somebody." So I was primed to go to college, and especially to attend a school away from home.

I would be remiss if I did not mention my gratitude to my parents and brother, Joe, who helped with my expenses during my 4 years at Hampton Institute. I told my mother several times that the values and principles she and my father instilled in me were as important, if not more so, than all my years of formal education.

During my childhood and formative years, I was often unhappy when my father said "No" when I wanted to do certain things or go to an out-of-town party. Years later, as I look back on those times, I was glad my parents were wise enough and cared enough to help keep me from harm.

What my parents taught us about how to relate to other people, regardless of their race, religion, or national origin, served me well in my years abroad as a young teacher in Liberia and throughout my career in education. I learned early on to respect my elders and not to take people for granted, and to treat others as I would like to be treated.

I am equally grateful to all those individuals who went out of their way to give me advice and help during my journey through life. They taught me a lot about paying it forward—like the little, elderly, indigenous, Liberian woman, who in 1961 brought me a bowl of rice because she worried that I was a long way from home and had no one to cook for me. That kind, selfless act touched me back then and even now. There were many others too numerous to name here.

As a classroom teacher for most of my career, I had the privilege of working with some of the most talented young people in the country and from around the world. As a history teacher, my focus was on the past and its relevance to current events. I recognized the inevitability and value of change and became a positive agent for new ideas and approaches. It was not always easy. The path forward was often nebulous, and I learned from mistakes. I must admit what most teachers realize is that so many of our students are savvier than we, and one of our tasks was to create opportunities to challenge and expand their intellectual curiosity.

Most of my classes were non-tracked, and some students faced problems due to background skills or lack of real interest in the topics under focus. I always tried to help them through the assigned work, but I insisted that they put forth a good effort. I truly cared about my students, advisees and athletes, as a mentor and a friend, but I maintained my proper distance as an adult.

I believe in standards, measuring points and helping young people to reach up, rather than lowering the pole. That sometimes led to awkward and uncomfortable situations. Students with mediocre performances and their parents occasionally took me to task over an average grade, but I stood firm.

In retrospect, I tried to make a difference in all the venues of my life. As a young IVS teacher/technician in Liberia, I made every effort to establish a working rapport with the people in the villages, while adhering to USAID/IVS policy. I established long lasting friendships with some of the students and African teachers I worked with.

In the two towns I lived and worked in, I contributed to building of two new schools, the training of new Liberian teachers and principals and improving international relations at the local level. I remain in contact with a few of my IVS team members, even though we only had one formal reunion, in 1968. We all agree that our two years in Liberia were some of our happiest times.

EXTENDED FAMILY OF
GEORGE N. DAVIS AND GERTRUDE (MINOR) DAVIS

VISITING RELATIVES IN CHATHAM, VIRGINIA

My brother Joe was not quite a year old when Mom and Dad made their first trip to Chatham to visit Gramma Linda. Grandad, Joe Henry, died before they arrived. He was 72 (1863-1935). We have photos of Gramma Linda, holding baby Joe. She came up to Scotch Plains in 1938 to spend time with her sister and Daddy, and his young family. We have a picture of her sitting on our lawn, facing Morse Avenue. I don't know how long she stayed, but I do know that Aunt Jenny's husband, Asa, was still living, because Momma told me how he used to hold me when I was a baby. Apparently, he could settle me down when I was upset.

Daddy took the family back to Chatham in 1940 or 41. Momma told me how relatives fawned over Joe and me as toddlers, with our curly red and blonde locks. Of course, I have no memory of this time, but Momma took photos of some family members, including Joe in Daddy's car, and Gramma Linda, Uncle Acie Dan and Aunts Sallie and Laura.

My first impression of "going down South" to visit Daddy's home was in 1947. We made the trip in his 1940 Plymouth 4-door sedan. I remember the endless fields of corn, tobacco and curing-barns, with the stovepipe chimneys, and the log cabins, with barefoot children playing on the red dirt.

Big trucks, loaded with logs, pick-up trucks carrying workers in the back who sat on the tailgates, and farmers riding big white horses and mules, made a big impression on me. The pungent smell of wood smoke was everywhere, and combined with the scent from curing tobacco, made the environment even more exotic and interesting. I was also surprised to see so many Black people along the roads and in the towns.

I can recall how the old farmhouse looked on the property. It was an old wooden house with a big chimney on each side. A roof covered porch faced the main road. The first floor consisted of a large family or living room, one bedroom and an eat-in kitchen and utility room.

On the second floor were two small bedrooms. I remember that the house looked in need of a paint job, repairs inside and out, and that the furniture was inadequate. As far as indoor plumbing or electric power, there was none at the time, as it would come much later. The old outhouse stood about 50 feet from the rear of the house. The freshwater spring was about 200 feet from the house, down a very steep hill, so it was quite a chore lugging a bucket of water up to the house, but the water was good.

Chickens walked about freely in the yard, and there was a corral for livestock near a barn, made of logs. There was a big wood chopping block with an axe stuck in its top and firewood lying around. A dirt driveway on both sides of the house joined at the rear and led out onto the property where the family cemetery was located, on the highest point. I had no idea that the farm was 120 acres, because we were not allowed to explore the areas far from the house. Everyone talked about snakes, and that was enough to scare me into compliance.

When we arrived, only Daddy's brother, Acie Dan, and his wife, Mary, and two young daughters, Clara Jean and Delores Lee, were living there. Acie and Mary would have 5 more children: Mariah, Lillian Ann, Shirley Temple, Katie; and one son, Acie Jr. Aunt Mary was a "Taylor," also from Chatham.

Across the road from our property stood the Ed Shelton farm. He owned over 250 acres, much of it planted with tobacco, wheat, corn and vegetables. He also raised chickens and pigs. Acie spoke highly of the Sheltons, and Daddy concurred. Our neighbors to the east and on the northern border were all white folk.

Our nearest Black neighbors were on Concord Road. It seemed like we were way out in the country, but our farm was just 3 miles west of the town of Chatham, where the train station and the main highway U.S. 29 were located. The city of Danville was 18 miles south, just near the North Carolina border.

There was a small store nearby on Concord Road that carried canned goods, bread, soda, candy and other items. Further down the road, there was another Black family-owned small shop that sold candy, soda and other goods. They were very industrious folks, and two of the daughters were college graduates. A lady named Miss Hannah taught in the one room schoolhouse that daddy attended. The family also had a nice farm.

Another Black farmer by the name of Carter, who we visited, had two big white horses and a mule, which he used to plow his fields. When we saw him, he was using crutches because he cut his leg on an old, buried piece of iron while plowing. I remember how bad his wounded calve looked. Daddy said he was a relative, and I later learned that my Great Grandmother was a Carter.

JOE HENRY DAVIS AND LINDA CRAFT DAVIS
AND CHILDREN

Joe Henry Davis was born in Pittsylvania County in 1863. His parents were Joe Davis and Jane Carter. Jane was likely an Indian (Indigenous American) who bore 5 children by a white slave owner named Carter before she married Joe. I don't know if the family was freed by the Emancipation Proclamation, issued by President Lincoln in January 1863, but I suspect that his father, Joe Davis, had been a slave in the western part of the county.

I don't have any evidence of Joe Henry's (my grandfather's) literacy, but I think he could read the Bible well enough to be a preacher. Local historians credit him as one of the founders of several churches in the Chatham area, including White Oak Grove Missionary Baptist on Dry Fork Road, Bannister River Baptist on SR 703, and Rosebud Baptist on Rosebud Street.

According to his contemporaries and others who knew him, Rev. Davis was a fine, God-fearing man. He also was a hard worker, good farmer, a loving father to his children and devoted husband. He got along well with his white neighbors and had gained their respect. Some of our neighbors who remembered him from their childhood commented on how "Uncle Joe" *used to help them harvest their crops,* and they in turn helped him. "We all got along well back then," according to neighboring families who shared with me.

According to Pittsylvania County marriage records, Joe Henry Davis was first married to a "Siney Davis" on January 17, 1882. He was 22, and she was 21 years old. They lived in the Tunstall District, where he owned land and paid taxes. They had children, but I don't know how many. One of these children, Rebecca Gatewood McClellan, brought a case in the Circuit Court in 1959, causing the property to be put up for auction. I don't know when Siney died.

Joe Henry remarried in 1901 to Linda Craft. He was listed as 38 years old and widowed, while Linda was 30. Apparently, they moved to Denora, Pennsylvania, where he found work in the mines, and their first child, Rebecca, was born there in 1902. A son, Joe, was also born, but he died of diphtheria at age 5. Both he and Rebecca are buried in the Davis family cemetery in Chatham.

In 1907—the year Rebecca died—Joe Henry purchased the 120-acre farm on SR 703 (now Irish Road). This property was formerly owned by a white family. According to my father and other relatives, the white husband was poisoned by his wife, who had discovered him having an affair. Although she apparently intended to kill herself and the children, one of the boys survived.

He lived and was thus the sole owner of the property, but he was too young to manage it. When the county treasurer, G.L. Carter, put the land up for auction, he accepted Joe Henry's bid of $1,200 for its purchase. We have the deed and receipts from the payments he made to settle the debt.

Joe Henry and Linda had 5 other children: Queen Esther, George Nelson, Sallie, Acie Dan and Laura. They all grew up on the farm in Chatham, and all are buried in the family cemetery, except for Esther, who was interred in Hampton, Virginia.

All the siblings married and moved away, except Acie Dan, who remained on the farm throughout his life. He took care of his mother, Linda, until her passing in 1943, during those difficult economic times. He farmed, cut pulpwood, and later worked at a furniture factory in Bassett.

Acie was a tall, handsome man who loved to dress up and court the ladies. He bought a Model T Ford so he and his buddies could cruise around the county, attending Baptist church association gatherings. Acie was a hard-working man, known for how fast he could cut up a load of pulpwood. Apparently, once while chopping wood, a chip bounced up and damaged his eye.

Queen Esther attended the Ingleside Seminary in Burkeville, Virginia, in 1922 for her secondary school training. She married Charlie Tarpley and had two sons, Bill and Jimmy, and they lived in Uniontown, Pennsylvania, until the marriage ended. She later married Ferdinand Early, from Uniontown, and they set up housekeeping in Hampton, Virginia. They lived with the McCallisters until they were able to buy their own home.

George Nelson, my father, moved up north to Scotch Plains, New Jersey, to live with his aunt Jenny while attending school. He remained in the area, marrying Gertrude Minor and raising 6 children: Joseph Henry, Gerald Nelson, George Dan, Nancy Ann, Lorraine Mae and JoAnn. All my siblings are alive at the time of this writing, except Nancy, who died of a brain tumor in 1962.

Sallie married Shirley Ramsey, from Gretna, Virginia, and they moved to Washington, D.C. They had 4 children: Joseph Lindbergh, Shirley Jr., Linda and David. Only Shirley Jr. and Linda are still alive.

Acie Dan married Mary Taylor, from Chatham, and they had 7 children: Clara Jean, Delores Lee, Mariah, Lillian Ann, Shirley, Acie Jr. and Katie. All except Delores are still alive.

Laura Lee was the youngest child. She lived in Washington D.C., but she eventually moved to New York City and married Johnny Jones. They adopted a baby boy, named Johnny. Laura died in 1955, and both her husband and son have since passed.

THE RICHARD DAVIS FAMILY IN CALLANDS

As I grew up, I gradually became aware of uncles, aunts and first cousins on Daddy's side, but there were many more Davises I didn't know about. I used to hear Daddy, Esther and Sallie refer to certain people as our kinfolk, but their exact relationship was never explained, or I was not listening carefully enough.

Joe Henry's brother, Richard Davis, was the oldest sibling, and he was born 1848. His wife, Martha, was probably born in 1857. Records indicate that they had 8 children: Leonard Son Davis, Flunory Risk Davis, Caroline Sim Davis, Florence Davis, Mary Davis, Lillie Bell Davis, Jenny Davis and Lucinda Davis. They were raised in Pittsylvania County, Virginia.

Daddy often spoke about his cousins, Spencer and Henry Davis, who he said were so light that they could "pass for white." In fact, he said that Spencer would deliberately hang around the whites sometimes and tell his relatives what they said. Their parents were Leonard (Son) Davis and Susie Wright; and their other siblings were Viola, Leonard Jr., Acie, Monroe, Richard and Virginia. They lived in the Callands community on Flint Hill Road.

Flunory (Risk) Davis, Leonard's younger brother, was married to Thelm Wright. They had 4 children: Daisy Bell, Harry, Phillis and Flunory Jr. They also lived in Callands.

James Davis, Joe Henry's other brother, was married to Mattie, and according to nephew Roy Banks Breedlove, James moved to Yanceyville or Reidsville, North Carolina. Their 6 children were Jim Orange Davis, Viola Davis, Uniecy Niecy Davis, Golden Davis, Evelenia Ting Davis and Helen Davis. (So far, I haven't met anyone from this wing of the family).

Emma and Sallie were Joe Henry's sisters. Emma Davis was married to Booker Breedlove, and they had 6 children: James, Richard, Roy (Banks), Joe, Willie and Evelyna. The lived in the Tunstall District. Sallie Davis married William Emmus Griggs, and they had 9 children: John Henry, Eddie Boyd, Joseph, William, Fannie, Mamie, Emily and Elizabeth. They also lived in the Tunstall District.

During my visits with my Aunt Sally Ramsey and Aunt Esther Early, I learned about my grandfather's siblings. When I was in Washington, D.C. I met Mamie Griggs Davis, who lived in Maryland. Aunt Esther told me that we were related to the Breedloves, and she introduced me to Vincent and Mary Ann Breedlove and their son Vincent Jr. (whom she took care of while Mary Ann worked). They lived in Hampton, Virginia, where I was attending Hampton University.

My father always spoke highly of Roy Banks Breedlove, and he took us to see him when we were younger. However, during those days I was not motivated to find out more about our kinship. Fortunately, I was able to visit Banks Breedlove at his home in Dry Fork on the occasion of his 100th birthday, at which time I leaned in to listen to his account of our extended family.

Also present at that occasion were Mr. Breedlove's wife and daughters. Evelyna, the youngest daughter, was married to Rev. Ross, and she was the executive director of the PCCA (Pittsylvania County Community Action Agency). She also has been elected vice president of the County NAACP Branch in Chatham.

JOE HENRY DAVIS, MY GRANDFATHER (1863-1935)

I was born in 1938, 3 years after my grandfather died. What I am writing here is based mainly on what others have told me about Joe Henry. Even though he was obviously a man of considerable stature in Chatham, there is little written information about him or his work. The family Bible and other papers that existed were lost in the 1981 fire that destroyed the family house on SR 703.

My Aunt Jenny was the first person I recall commenting on Joe Henry, whom she referred to as "Brother Davis." She said Joe Henry preached at St. John's Baptist Church at a revival. I don't recall if Aunt Jenny said his wife, Linda, was with him, and I don't know what year it was; but she said that he preached a powerful sermon that drew lots of "Amens."

She also said that he was not a person to mince his words. He spoke frankly, and he occasionally used profanity and "earthy language." Like most preachers, he admonished his congregation about their sins. To the women in the front row pews, he would warn, "Don't sit up here, showing your underwear." To the men, he advised them to treat their "wives and children kindly, and make sure they attend church and follow the teachings of the Bible." He did not approve of excessive drinking and drunkenness.

Aunt Jenny said that he was a good husband who helped his wife with household chores and with canning food for the winter months. He was a hands-on farmer, planting tobacco as his cash crop, as well as wheat, corn, beans, squash, pumpkins, sweet potatoes, tomatoes and other vegetables. He had peach, apple, pear, cherry and persimmon trees—some of which are still producing. He raised hogs, chickens, and he had a milking cow, horses and mules.

Daddy said it took "Papa" all day to deliver a load of cured tobacco to the warehouse in Danville; but he usually bought some candy or sweets for the kids. Because he was a preacher, Joe Henry attended most of the Baptist church association gatherings. Those were both religious and social get-togethers, which involved all church members and their families who could attend.

The women brought home-cooked meals and desserts and enjoyed those opportunities to meet and greet other folks from county towns. The preachers, deacons and other important church dignitaries were recognized, and Daddy said "Papa" was always one of the preachers to be asked to deliver the opening prayer or benediction.

Joe Henry was also adept at telling stories and jokes, which Daddy shared with us, like the one about a man who outran a quarter horse to show that he should be hired. Then there was the story about a man trying to outrun a ghost, or the reaction of a preacher giving a eulogy when the body in the open casket suddenly sat up.

The photos we have of Joe Henry Davis and Linda Craft Davis show them to be a very handsome couple. He was quite fair, with fine hair and keen features. He was of average height (5' 10") and well-built. Gramma Linda was also fair in complexion and had reddish hair that was coarser. She and Aunt Jenny looked very much alike. From the photos, she looks more thoughtful and serious than happy.

Joe Henry was born in 1863 as slavery was coming to its dramatic and violent end during the bloody Civil War. It is not clear exactly where he was born, but court and tax records indicate that he more than likely grew up in the southwestern part of Pittsylvania County, or Henry County.

The town of Axton, about 15 miles west of Danville, is home to a lot of Davises, who are relatives of one degree or another. Tax records I have indicate that he paid taxes in the Tunstall District in the 1880s and 1890s. He raised tobacco, like most farmers. Some of his brothers and sisters lived in the immediate area and in nearby Dry Fork.

Joe Henry's parents, Joe Davis and Jane (Carter) Davis, are listed in Pittsylvania County court marriage records in 1882. Records indicate that they were also the parents of Richard Davis, James Davis, Emma (Davis) Breedlove, and Sally (Davis) Griggs. So far, I have been unable to find their burial site.

THE CRAFTS AND OTHER RELATIVES IN NEW JERSEY

My hometown, Scotch Plains, New Jersey, or more specifically, "Jerseyland," was a community where other families with roots in Pittsylvania County, Virginia, had settled. The Lipfords, Womacks and Pruntys were from southside Virginia. Relatives told me that we were related to the Pruntys, and I remember "cousin" Carrie Prunty and her sons, who lived on Jerusalem Road. Daddy often stopped to visit them and Mrs. Pugh, who lived next door.

Another family we were related to, the Smiths, also lived in Jerseyland. Sunny and Fannie Smith had at least 8 children, and they lived on Turney Avenue. Sunny was short, thin and of light complexion. Fannie was also fair, but of a heavier build. Both had fine, dark wavy hair, as did their children. The oldest child, Trottley, could pass for white, but the other siblings were accurately described as "mulattoes," or Indians. There was Dudley, Ezekiel, Kelsey, Otha, Quella, Luella and Aleece. They were all much older than me, but I do remember some of them.

Ezekiel was known for shooting a cigarette from his brother's mouth with a 22. Rifle. Trottley was said to hold a younger brother over the well by his ankles and drop and then catch him. The last time I saw Trottley was when he came back home and stopped by to see my father in the 1950s. He was living in Missouri. Dudley worked with Daddy and me clearing a wood lot in Scotch Plains on Front Street. He built a house on Smith Street, next to the Community Center. When I was in high school, I met Lorlei Adams, and for a time we hung out together. She was the daughter of Quella and Tee Adams.

When I retired and moved to Chatham in 2000, I discovered a letter that Fannie Smith wrote to her husband, Sunny. It was postmarked from Gretna, Virginia. Apparently, this letter was in my Aunt Jenny's papers, which my father retained after she died in 1960. Quella and Tee Adams came down to spend time with my parents in Chatham after Daddy retired and moved back home.

There was an older lady named Angeline Craft who lived near us on Plainfield Avenue in Scotch Plains. I remember looking after her, running errands and keeping her company. I never knew her husband, but I remember well her adopted son Harold, his wife Amelia, and their children, Janet, Harold, and Connie.

Once when I was being a jerk, teasing Connie, Harold Sr., a special policeman, handcuffed me to the bedpost, and I stayed there until he came home from work. Amelia died, and Harold remarried and moved to Keyport, New Jersey, where he found employment as a chef. Harold Jr. became a tour bus driver and occasionally stopped by to visit old friends and family in Jerseyland.

Jim and Susie Craft and their sons, Richard and Howard, lived in Plainfield on Cottage Street. Daddy told us how they were forced to flee from their home in Chatham when they were threatened by racists who wanted their farm. According to Daddy, there were some white men who claimed that Jim's deed to his farm was illegitimate, and they tried to run him and Susie off their land. When Jim complained to the county sheriff, the sheriff replied that he would have to "protect himself."

Consequently, he and Susie did just that, resulting in a shoot-out one night on their property. When it was over, a few white men were shot, and under the cover of night, Jim and Susie rode into Chatham and caught the 2 a.m. train heading north. They eventually settled safely in Plainfield, New Jersey. I am sure they were related to my grandmother, Linda Craft, or to the Davises in Chatham. I remember visiting them in Plainfield with Daddy.

I had heard the story of one Jack Craft, who lived in the mountains near Beckley, West Virginia. He was related to my grandmother Linda's family who lived in that area. Daddy described him as an outlaw who committed robbery and hid out in the mountains. He wore a pair of 32/20 pistols and would not hesitate to use them.

Daddy recalled those stories with obvious relish, because he was proud of how those men stood up to the racist establishment. He also told us about an "Uncle Jim," who had been a slave and who apparently was brave and smart enough to sneak around the county to visit other slaves, in violation of his master's rules. He somehow got someone to write out a pass or a letter of permission from his master, which he used occasionally.

Our family's experience with another relative was not so positive. In the post WWII period, 1947-1953, one relative came to stay with us in Scotch Plains for a while. He was supposed to be looking for employment, but he discovered where Daddy kept his savings locked up, and he stole about $1,000.00 and fled.

I was too young to remember much about him, but I do know he was a charmer, like con men tend to be. Daddy never recovered his hard-earned savings, despite the young man's father promising to return the money. This experience made my father suspicious of anyone coming into our house, or of us "bothering" any of his personal things.

I can still see the desk at the top of the stairs where the money was stored with the padlock, which had been pried loose with a claw hammer. Daddy may not have reported the theft, hoping that the money would be returned. I don't know whether Daddy ever heard from that relative again.

THE MINORS, THE MUSES AND THE STEWARTS

My mother, Gertrude Minor, was one of 7 children born to Florida Minor in the small town of Cumnor, in King and Queen County, Virginia. Florida apparently worked for a white family who owned a store and adjoining land. She stayed in the back of the store. Two of her children were fathered by the son of her employer. Momma and her sister Ivory were light-skinned and had long fine dark hair, while all the other siblings were dark with coarse hair.

Momma always felt a degree of shame about her mother's circumstance, and about how it affected her relationship with her brothers and sisters.

Robert Minor, the oldest child, came to stay with us in Scotch Plains in 1953. He and his family lived in South Jersey, and he was looking for work in construction. I remember him more clearly, especially his manner of speaking and the stories of his youth in Virginia.

When his mother died, he was taken in by a man who was very strict and cruel. When he did anything wrong, he was hung up by his wrists and whipped by this man, who was a relative. Eventually, Robert ran away and made a life for himself. He and his wife had several children while living in South Jersey. Their twin girls kept in touch with my mother, and after she passed, I spoke with one on the phone, who lived in Boston.

Momma's older sister, Winnie, with whom she was close, was married to David Muse, who was also from King and Queen County, Virginia. They had two children, Roosevelt and Alberta, and they lived in Westfield, New Jersey. Uncle David was a kind man who I remember took the time to spend with us kids, making us feel welcome. Unfortunately, he died too early. Aunt Winnie, who learned to drive and always had her own car, often traveled back to Virginia to see the folks who raised her and spent time with me, my siblings and our children at family gatherings. She lived to the age of 92.

Reginald Minor was another brother. He moved up to Philadelphia and served in the military during WWII. I never had any contact with him. He was 95 when he died. Edward Minor was younger than Momma, and he also lived in Philadelphia. He came over to visit us on several occasions, and he and Momma corresponded regularly. He was a handyman, a cabinet-maker and a good cook. On the last occasion he visited us in Scotch Plains, he brought his lady friend.

Thomas Minor (Bagby) was also younger than Momma. He lived in Petersburg, Virginia, and had a daughter I never met. He came to visit Momma and Daddy in Chatham once before Daddy died, and he came to Daddy's funeral. The last visit he made was in 2001, but he was very frail then. We were not notified of his passing.

Ivory Minor was older than Momma, and she also lived in the Philadelphia area. She had children, but I don't know anything about them. She enjoyed life but also died too soon.

Ella Minor was the youngest sibling. She was living in Cumnor and working. She and Momma corresponded often, and I found some of her letters after Momma died. Daddy took us to Bordentown to visit Cousin Nancy a few times. She lived in her own home with her husband and son. She kept a neat house, was a stickler for cleanliness and her yard had flowers and grapes. She did domestic work for white families. Her husband was disabled and didn't work outside of the home.

Momma said that before she went to live with Cousin Nancy, she was staying with another relative and his wife and son. One day, she and the boy were cutting wood with an axe—instead of the saw—which made the patriarch of the family angry. He began whipping Momma with a big switch because she had disobeyed him. He hit her on the head several times, drawing blood, until his wife screamed at him to stop. After such treatment, she was happy to go home with Nancy Stewart.

When my mom first arrived at her cousin's home in Bordentown after her attack in her previous residence, she faced resentment and jealously for the attention she received from her cousin's son, which included a time when he hit her on the head with a stick or a blunt object, re-opening an old wound that caused a lifelong sore spot. Fortunately, they eventually learned to get along.

As a devout Christian, Cousin Nancy regularly attended church, and she was a no-nonsense person. She moved quickly and spoke clearly and meant what she said. Momma loved her and always felt beholden to her.

When I started driving in 1955, I took Momma, Lorraine and JoAnn to visit the Stewarts in Bordentown. When I graduated from Hampton University in 1961, I stopped in Bordentown for an overnight with the Stewarts. With my car was loaded down with luggage and ceramics, I needed a rest. Cousin Nancy was thrilled that I was going to Liberia, West Africa, to teach. The last time I visited them was after I got married in 1965-66.

ESTHER AND FERD EARLY
AND THE BREEDLOVES IN HAMPTON, VIRGINIA

After I graduated from high school in 1957, I decided to attend Hampton University in Hampton, Virginia. My decision was influenced by my Aunt Esther and her husband, Ferd Early, who lived there. They spoke highly of the school and encouraged me to come down for a visit. My brother Joe drove us down in his brand new 1956 Ford, and we had a great time touring the campus, including Fort Monroe, where Ferd worked, and Langley Air Force Base

I'm glad I had the chance to live in a community of educated Black people, where I was happier than I would have been if I had chosen to attend Rutgers. I enjoyed the comfort of Aunt Esther's home, even though I lived on campus. I made the right decision, spending 4 of the happiest years of my life at Hampton, right on the Chesapeake Bay.

Aunt Esther was Daddy's oldest sister, which I didn't know at that time. He had spent time with her in Uniontown, Pennsylvania, when she was married to Charlie Tarpley. She valued education and was proud of the time she attended Ingleside Seminary. Strong-willed, she was domineering and a very devout Christian who, like her siblings, was easily excitable and emotional. On the home front, she was an excellent housekeeper, a good cook and hostess. She and Ferd were raising their grandson, who suffered from a cleft palate, which required several surgeries that they paid for.

Esther had two sons by her first husband: Bill, and Jimmy. They grew up in Uniontown, but they had moved to the Tidewater area after time in the Army. Bill was married to Claire, and they had 4 children: Martel, Barbara, Sharon and Richard. Jimmy and wife, Lorraine, moved to New Port News with their son, Charles. I spent time with both families during my time at Hampton.

Bill worked in the Post Office in Hampton and was an accomplished artist. He spent time at Hampton University's Art department, painting in watercolors and oil, and he was also a pottery buff. I have one of his oil paintings in my house now. He became an ordained Minister later in life. At my father's funeral in 1983, Bill offered a moving eulogy. He and Claire still reside at their home on Elm St in Hampton.

Uncle Ferd was a carpenter/cabinetmaker by trade and was a federal employee at Fort Monroe, with a daughter from a previous marriage. A jovial, friendly, happy man, he was always fun to be around. As a youth during the Great Depression, he was a hobo for a time, traveling across the country. Thus, he had a lot of tales to share, such as his explanation about how he started chewing tobacco when he met a girl in Tennessee who he later discovered dipped snuff. He said he decided to try it himself to get close to her!

When Esther and Ferd moved to Hampton after WWII, they rented an apartment at Dr. McCallister's house on King Street. He was the school dentist at Hampton. When they could afford it, they purchased their own house on nearby Union Street. It was beautifully furnished, and Esther kept it clean and neat inside. Their yard had many pretty flowers, a neatly mowed lawn, and in the rear was Ferd's shop.

He drove a Plymouth, but Esther did not drive (except from the back seat!). After I left Hampton, a gentrification project caused all the Union Street houses to be demolished, to be replaced by a housing project. Ferd and Esther then bought a nice ranch-style house on New Port News Avenue.

Aunt Esther broadened my knowledge of our relatives. She spoke a lot about "Papa" and her siblings. She told me how hard Daddy worked as a boy, plowing with the mules. "Papa" would tell young George in jest, "Boy take it easy on those mules. Put them in the shade for a spell." She also said that "Papa" and "Momma" were strict on her, Sally and Laura. Local boys knew they had to step lightly and show a proper reverence and respect when they came to visit.

Esther told me about the Breedloves in Chatham, and she introduced me to Vincent and Mary Ann Breedlove, who lived in Hampton. She took care of their little son, Vince Jr., while Mary Ann worked. It was never clear how closely we were related, but I suppose I didn't ask enough questions at the time. The last time I saw them was at Esther's funeral in Hampton, in 1985. Ferd preceded her in death.

GERALD, GALE AND CHANNING DAVIS: CHATHAM RESIDENTS

I retired from teaching at Northfield Mount Hermon School in June 2000. After 3-plus decades at that wonderful school, Gale and I were ready to move on to the next chapter of our lives. Our oldest son Channing, who had been working in the dining Hall at NMH, moved with us. His brother, Sterling, who graduated from NMH and Emerson College, was working in Hollywood, California, at the American Film Institute. He is a photographer, graphic designer, and he works on various TV shows as an editor.

One of the reasons I wanted to relocate to Chatham was to be near Momma, who was 87 and living independently in the nice single-wide my father purchased in 1976 when he retired. I drove him and my sister JoAnn to Chatham, where Daddy met his lawyer to finalize his deed and arrange for the upcoming move. Daddy bought a beautifully equipped Oakwood home, fully-furnished and ready to move in. My brother Joe and his wife Shirley accompanied them on their trip south. Daddy's big Dodge station wagon was overloaded, resulting in flat tires and other problems, but they made it safely.

Gale, the boys and I enjoyed our annual trips south, stopping in Chatham for a few days before driving on down to Columbus, Georgia, to see Gale's family. Daddy walked us around the property, down through the low grounds, pointing out who our neighbors were. Though his health was failing, he made some improvements on the property.

He cleared a space for a garden down by the spring and created a small pool by blocking up the creek. It was a nice place to sit during the heat of the day. Since he stopped his brother from cutting pulpwood, the trees had grown considerably, except for on the tobacco fields he leased out to Giles, a farmer who lived nearby. The money he gained from the lease was practically enough to cover the annual tax bill.

From 1976 until Daddy died in August 1983, he and Momma entertained family and friends who visited. Acie Dan, his wife Mary, Acie Jr. and his wife Mable and their children had been living in the old house, until Acie Jr. bought a trailer in 1976. After the house burned down in

1981, Acie Dan and Mary moved in with Acie Jr. and Mable. All that
remained of the house were the two big chimneys. Daddy was very upset
over the loss of the old homestead.

Acie and Mary's other children, Clara Jean, Delores, Mariah, Lillian
Ann, Shirley and Katie were married or living elsewhere in the county.
Anne, her husband, Leonard Craft, and son, Darius, lived in Gretna.
Delores and her husband, Connie, and daughters lived in Penhook; Mariah
got married and had several children. Shirley had a daughter, JoAnn.
Katie, and the youngest had a daughter, Krystal, and she eventually
married P. L. Leftwich of Whitmell. Clara, the oldest, was married to
Leonard Adkins, and they lived in Danville. They had children, but I don't
know their names.

I am sorry that I never had the opportunity to get to know Delores as an
adult. I learned that she suffered a tragic loss when her daughter died in a
house fire in Penhook. She never quite got over the accident. Her husband,
Connie, was a logger who died in a workplace accident.

BUYING A HOME AND MOVING

We had never purchased a house, because we lived at a school that
provided us with free housing and meals. Since 1973, we were living in a
nice brick house with a two-car garage and full basement on campus. So
we had so much stuff to dispose of and pack up for the move.

Fortunately, we found ABF who provided a 28-foot. trailer which we
loaded. They picked it up and drove it to our new home, a 28 x 60-foot
Fleetwood double-wide on the family property in Chatham. Actually, we
arrived in Chatham on the 1st of July 2000, after an overnight in Silver
Spring, Maryland, with Gale's sister, Rosalind. I drove my Ford F-150
truck, loaded down, while Channing drove our '92 Honda Accord with
Gale.

My brothers, Joe and Danny, were in Chatham when the ABF truck
arrived, so they helped us unload the trailer. The home had been here since
1995, but it was unfurnished, except for two beds and a couple chairs. The
kitchen had a refrigerator and stove, and we soon bought a washer/dryer.
We had been staying here during our visits since it was set up. It was great
having central air. I built a 10 x10-foot deck in the front, and later another
one in the back, with a roof. Channing and I built a 12 x16-foot shed to
house our tools and other items, and we eventually we put up another shed,
with Joe's help, to hold our riding mower and other lawn tools.

Joe had a Jim Walters home built on the same lot where the old house
stood. He knocked down the chimneys and cleared away the debris, and

the house was 60 percent completed by 1991. He finished the interior with help from friends in New Jersey and from family members.

Channing and I helped with hanging sheet rock and with the foundation. He had not moved there, but he came down to work on the house and spend time with Momma. After Gale, Channing and I moved, he began to spend more time here.

By 2002, he had become a permanent resident. His wife, Shirley, remained in Plainfield, New Jersey, but she came down to visit. Joe regularly drove back to see Shirley and their children.

MEETING PEOPLE AND LEARNING THE ENVIRONMENT

Since Momma didn't drive or have a car, she spent most of her time at home. Mable took her shopping for groceries, and Milo Simmons and his sister, Hannah Fuller, also included her on their trips to Chatham or Danville. Hannah was in her 90s, but she was living alone in her home on Concord Road. Milo, a few years younger, also lived on the Simmons' farm in his own trailer.

I recall walking with Momma and our two boys to visit Hannah and her brothers, Richard, and Milo, in the 1980s. Richard was about 95, but he was spry and opinionated. He criticized Acie Dan for not taking better advantage of his opportunity. Richard owned a 1959 Chevy pickup, which he kept in the garage.

Since he stopped driving, the truck was seldom used, and eventually, after he passed, Milo tried to sell it. He had a 1955 Ford sedan which he kept in running order. Hannah's other sisters lived in Pennsylvania and Washington, D.C. Doris, the one who lived in D.C., built a beautiful brick house, across the street from Hannah. She was a good friend of Aunt Sally.

WILMER AND MARY FITZGERALD FAMILY

Mr. Wilmer Fitzgerald stopped by our house for a visit one Sunday afternoon in the summer of 2000. He and his wife, Mary, were old friends of my father. Wilmer was a tobacco farmer who owned over 100 acres on Route 57. He raised a crop of tobacco on our land and paid Daddy $400. Mary's maiden name was "Price," and two of her brothers were Clarence and Carl, Daddy's childhood buddies. He told me how he gave Mary his coat one winter day because she didn't have one walking home from the schoolhouse.

As a moral to the story, Mary called Daddy in 1959 to let him know that our homestead was to be auctioned off because of unpaid taxes. Consequently, as mentioned before, Daddy and Joe rushed down there and stopped the auction. Even though, he shared ownership of the farm with his siblings, Acie Dan, Sallie, Esther and Laura—Daddy was the steward of the property and paid the taxes, and he later became sole owner.

Wilmer and Mary lived in a nice two-story white house on Route 57. They had 8 children: Florence, Wilmer Jr. (Young), Lee, Allan, Aubrey, Doris, Faye and Phillis. I became acquainted with them through time spent in Washington D.C. with Aunt Sally and Uncle Shirley Ramsey.

Their daughter, Linda, married Young, who was an Army Lieutenant stationed near D.C. He graduated from Virginia State College and its ROTC program, and he endured two tours in Vietnam. He was the one I mentioned switching places with so that he could join his bride at the hotel. While in the barracks, I was dumped from the bunk by his buddies in the middle of the night who thought I was him.

Linda and Young had 4 daughters: Cherie, Cherae, Cherelle and Chantell. Like other "military brats," they experienced growing up in several different environments, including South Korea, Italy, Japan, Germany and the U.S. Their permanent home was in Oxen Hill, Maryland. All graduated from college, married, had children and settled in the D.C./Virginia area.

Young retired as a Lt. Colonel, and he was employed by the Scientific and Commercial systems Corporation (SCSC) as division director of Fabrication and Assembly, and he was promoted to vice president of that Division in Falls Church, VA. He and Linda were generous hosts to extended family and friends over the years. Before he died in April 2003, he and Linda were actively planning to build a new home in Chatham. His mother, Mary, had passed, but his father was still living on his farm.

Young was buried in our family cemetery on Irish Road, behind my house. Also resting there are his brother-in-law, David Ramsey, Aunt Sallie and Uncle Shirley Ramsey. Aubrey Fitzgerald Jones, Doris Fitzgerald, and Phillis Fitzgerald Winston have since moved back home to Chatham and regularly visit their brother's gravesite. Doris took care of her father, Wilmer Sr., at her home on Main Street until his passing in 2008 at age 100.

ROY BANKS BREEDLOVE AND FAMILY

One of Daddy's childhood friends whom he talked about often was a man he called "Banks." On our trip to Chatham in 1976, we visited Roy (Banks) and Lucy Breedlove at their home in Dry Fork. I recall Banks telling the story of a young doctor whose father took a vacation and left him to care for his patients. When his father returned, the son told him how he had cured an old lady. His father was upset and told him that it was "patients like her" who had paid his way through medical school.

Banks' sight was beginning to fail him, but he continued to do what chores he could around the house. Lucy was quiet, but she was a pleasant host to us. At that time, I didn't know specifically how we were related to Roy Breedlove.

I later learned that Banks' mother, Emma, was Joe Henry's sister. She was fair in complexion with dark, wavy hair. Her husband, Booker Breedlove, was a handsome man of average height with a dark complexion. Their other children were Willie, Evelyna and James.

Banks and Lucy had two daughters: Lillie Kate Breedlove and Evelyna Breedlove Ross. Evelyna and her husband, Larry Ross, live next door to the house Banks and Lucy lived on SR 703. Larry Ross is the pastor at Rosebud Church in Chatham. Evelyna works for the County Community Action Committee and is the vice president of the county NAACP. I met her sister, Lillie, in 2006 at the Breedlove home at a family gathering. She lives in Forestville, Maryland.

When Roy Banks Breedlove turned 100, his family and friends had a big celebration party. I did not attend the affair, but Gale, Channing and I joined some others on a visit to the Breedlove home. Linda Fitzgerald, Aubrey Jones, Ronald Davis, my brother Joe, Walter Breedlove and Bank's daughters were there.

Banks sat in his recliner, but he spoke with us, answering questions about our genealogy. He was practically blind at that point. His family put together a nice color brochure with photos and short bio sketches. When Banks died in August 2007, the local media published articles about him, and CRISIS magazine, the NAACP publication, followed up with a nice complementary piece.

Banks' daughters and other family members established a scholarship fund in his name for a deserving high school graduate. Though he never finished high school, Banks insisted that his daughters go to college. He was well-known in the community for his support to those young people who were trying to get an education. His daughter, Evelyna, said that "despite the problems he encountered, like losing an eye in an accident while a boy and suffering from racial discrimination," he maintained an optimism that all who knew him recognized and saw as inspiration.

SALLY JANE DAVIS AND WILLIAM EMMUS GRIGGS

During the times I spent with Aunt Sally and Uncle Shirley Ramsey in Washington D.C., I met "Cousin" Mamie (Griggs) Davis, who lived in Silver Spring, Maryland. She had a son named Ronald, who was 4 years older than me. I only learned of how we were related when I began to research our family genealogy.

I'm not sure when I last saw Mamie, but it was probably at a funeral in Chatham. She survived her sister, Emily Griggs Adams, and probably attended the latter's funeral. Emily left her home on Mt. Cross Road near Danville. Ronald Davis had to come down from D.C. on a couple of occasions to arrange for repairs to the property. He stopped by my house on one of these visits, but I was asleep, having been up all night on the job. Ronald died on May 4, 2010, in Washington D.C. He was survived by two children, Donna and Ryan, but was predeceased by his wife. I never met his wife or children.

Emily Griggs married Samuel Adams in 1935. They raised Mary Elizabeth Burks, daughter of Daniel and Delsia Adams. Sam was a member of Piney Grove Primitive Baptist Church. He worked at Dan River Mills, Danville, for 40 years, and was known for his skills as a hunter. Emily was a member of Holbrook Street Presbyterian Church United, and a domestic worker. Samuel died in 1989 and Emily died in 2005, at 93. I never met them, but found this information in "Family Wisdom," (2006) written by Howard G. Adams, PH. D.

William Howard Taft Griggs (son of Sally Jane) and wife Martha had two children: William Gerald and Donna. William (married Marva), and they had two children, Anthony and Katrina.

Anthony was born on February 12, 1960, in Lawton, Ohio. As a professional football player, he was a linebacker with the Philadelphia Eagles (1982-85) and the Cleveland Browns (1986-88). His NFL career began as a fourth-round draft pick for the Eagles in 1982, out of Ohio State. However, he graduated with a B.A. degree in Communications from Villanova in 1983.

After his playing career was over, Anthony joined the Pittsburgh Steelers in 1992 to work in player programs. His responsibilities included continuing education, internships, investment information and counseling services for players. He also assisted the conditioning coordinator with strength programs for players. He is married with two children. This information on the Griggs family is attributed to an unpublished genealogy on the Davis/Carter family of Pittsylvania County, Virginia.

Part Seven

EXTENDED FAMILY OF
GEORGE N. DAVIS AND GERTRUDE (MINOR) DAVIS

VISITING RELATIVES IN CHATHAM, VIRGINIA

My brother, Joe, was not quite a year old when Mom and Dad made their first trip to Chatham to visit Gramma Linda. Grandad, Joe Henry, died before they arrived. He was 72 (1863-1935). We have photos of Gramma Linda, holding baby Joe. She came up to Scotch Plains in 1938 to spend time with her sister and Daddy, and his young family. We have a picture of her sitting on our lawn, facing Morse Avenue. I don't know how long she stayed, but I do know that Aunt Jenny's husband, Asa, was still living, because Momma told me how he used to hold me when I was a baby. Apparently, he could settle me down when I was upset.

Daddy took the family back to Chatham in 1940 or 41. Momma told me how relatives fawned over Joe and me as toddlers, with our curly red and blonde locks. Of course, I have no memory of this time, but Momma took photos of some family members, including Joe in Daddy's car, and Gramma Linda, Uncle Acie Dan and Aunts Sallie and Laura.

My first impression of "going down South" to visit Daddy's home was in 1947. We made the trip in his 1940 Plymouth 4-door sedan. I remember the endless fields of corn, tobacco and curing-barns, with the stovepipe chimneys, and the log cabins, with barefoot children playing on the red dirt.

Big trucks, loaded with logs, pick-up trucks carrying workers in the back who sat on the tailgates, and farmers riding big white horses and mules, made a big impression on me. The pungent smell of wood smoke was everywhere, and combined with the scent from curing tobacco, made the environment even more exotic and interesting. I was also surprised to see so many Black people along the roads and in the towns.

I can recall how the old farmhouse looked on the property. It was an old wooden house with a big chimney on each side. A roof covered porch faced the main road. The first floor consisted of a large family or living room, one bedroom and an eat-in kitchen and utility room.

On the second floor were two small bedrooms. I remember that the house looked in need of a paint job, repairs inside and out, and that the furniture was inadequate. As far as indoor plumbing or electric power, there was none at the time, as it would come much later. The old outhouse stood about 50 feet from the rear of the house. The freshwater spring was about 200 feet from the house, down a very steep hill, so it was quite a chore lugging a bucket of water up to the house, but the water was good.

Chickens walked about freely in the yard, and there was a corral for livestock near a barn, made of logs. There was a big wood chopping block with an axe stuck in its top and firewood lying around. A dirt driveway on both sides of the house joined at the rear and led out onto the property where the family cemetery was located, on the highest point. I had no idea that the farm was 120 acres, because we were not allowed to explore the areas far from the house. Everyone talked about snakes, and that was enough to scare me into compliance.

When we arrived, only Daddy's brother, Acie Dan, and his wife, Mary, and two young daughters, Clara Jean and Delores Lee, were living there. Acie and Mary would have 5 more children: Mariah, Lillian Ann, Shirley Temple, Katie; and one son, Acie Jr. Aunt Mary was a "Taylor," also from Chatham.

Across the road from our property stood the Ed Shelton farm. He owned over 250 acres, much of it planted with tobacco, wheat, corn and vegetables. He also raised chickens and pigs. Acie spoke highly of the Sheltons, and Daddy concurred. Our neighbors to the east and on the northern border were all white folk.

Our nearest Black neighbors were on Concord Road. It seemed like we were way out in the country, but our farm was just 3 miles west of the town of Chatham, where the train station and the main highway U.S. 29 were located. The city of Danville was 18 miles south, just near the North Carolina border.

There was a small store nearby on Concord Road that carried canned goods, bread, soda, candy and other items. Further down the road, there was another Black family-owned small shop that sold candy, soda and other goods. They were very industrious folks, and two of the daughters were college graduates. A lady named Miss Hannah taught in the one room schoolhouse that daddy attended. The family also had a nice farm.

Another Black farmer by the name of Carter, who we visited, had two big white horses and a mule, which he used to plow his fields. When we saw him, he was using crutches because he cut his leg on an old, buried piece of iron while plowing. I remember how bad his wounded calve looked. Daddy said he was a relative, and I later learned that my Great Grandmother was a Carter.

JOE HENRY DAVIS AND LINDA CRAFT DAVIS
AND CHILDREN

Joe Henry Davis was born in Pittsylvania County in 1863. His parents were Joe Davis and Jane Carter. Jane was likely an Indian (Indigenous American) who bore 5 children by a white slave owner named Carter before she married Joe. I don't know if the family was freed by the Emancipation Proclamation, issued by President Lincoln in January 1863, but I suspect that his father, Joe Davis, had been a slave in the western part of the county.

I don't have any evidence of Joe Henry's (my grandfather's) literacy, but I think he could read the Bible well enough to be a preacher. Local historians credit him as one of the founders of several churches in the Chatham area, including White Oak Grove Missionary Baptist on Dry Fork Road, Bannister River Baptist on SR 703, and Rosebud Baptist on Rosebud Street.

According to his contemporaries and others who knew him, Rev. Davis was a fine, God-fearing man. He also was a hard worker, good farmer, a loving father to his children and devoted husband. He got along well with his white neighbors and had gained their respect. Some of our neighbors who remembered him from their childhood commented on how "Uncle Joe" *used to help them harvest their crops,* and they in turn helped him. "We all got along well back then," according to neighboring families who shared with me.

According to Pittsylvania County marriage records, Joe Henry Davis was first married to a "Siney Davis" on January 17, 1882. He was 22, and she was 21 years old. They lived in the Tunstall District, where he owned land and paid taxes. They had children, but I don't know how many. One of these children, Rebecca Gatewood McClellan, brought a case in the Circuit Court in 1959, causing the property to be put up for auction. I don't know when Siney died.

Joe Henry remarried in 1901 to Linda Craft. He was listed as 38 years old and widowed, while Linda was 30. Apparently, they moved to Denora, Pennsylvania, where he found work in the mines, and their first child, Rebecca, was born there in 1902. A son, Joe, was also born, but he died of diphtheria at age 5. Both he and Rebecca are buried in the Davis family cemetery in Chatham.

In 1907—the year Rebecca died—Joe Henry purchased the 120-acre farm on SR 703 (now Irish Road). This property was formerly owned by a white family. According to my father and other relatives, the white husband was poisoned by his wife, who had discovered him having an affair. Although she apparently intended to kill herself and the children, one of the boys survived.

He lived and was thus the sole owner of the property, but he was too young to manage it. When the county treasurer, G.L. Carter, put the land up for auction, he accepted Joe Henry's bid of $1,200 for its purchase. We have the deed and receipts from the payments he made to settle the debt.

Joe Henry and Linda had 5 other children: Queen Esther, George Nelson, Sallie, Acie Dan and Laura. They all grew up on the farm in Chatham, and all are buried in the family cemetery, except for Esther, who was interred in Hampton, Virginia.

All the siblings married and moved away, except Acie Dan, who remained on the farm throughout his life. He took care of his mother, Linda, until her passing in 1943, during those difficult economic times. He farmed, cut pulpwood, and later worked at a furniture factory in Bassett.

Acie was a tall, handsome man who loved to dress up and court the ladies. He bought a Model T Ford so he and his buddies could cruise around the county, attending Baptist church association gatherings. Acie was a hard-working man, known for how fast he could cut up a load of pulpwood. Apparently, once while chopping wood, a chip bounced up and damaged his eye.

Queen Esther attended the Ingleside Seminary in Burkeville, Virginia, in 1922 for her secondary school training. She married Charlie Tarpley and had two sons, Bill and Jimmy, and they lived in Uniontown, Pennsylvania, until the marriage ended. She later married Ferdinand Early, from Uniontown, and they set up housekeeping in Hampton, Virginia. They lived with the McCallisters until they were able to buy their own home.

George Nelson, my father, moved up north to Scotch Plains, New Jersey, to live with his aunt Jenny while attending school. He remained in the area, marrying Gertrude Minor and raising 6 children: Joseph Henry, Gerald Nelson, George Dan, Nancy Ann, Lorraine Mae and JoAnn. All my siblings are alive at the time of this writing, except Nancy, who died of a brain tumor in 1962.

Sallie married Shirley Ramsey, from Gretna, Virginia, and they moved to Washington, D.C. They had 4 children: Joseph Lindbergh, Shirley Jr., Linda and David. Only Shirley Jr. and Linda are still alive.

Acie Dan married Mary Taylor, from Chatham, and they had 7 children: Clara Jean, Delores Lee, Mariah, Lillian Ann, Shirley, Acie Jr. and Katie. All except Delores are still alive.

Laura Lee was the youngest child. She lived in Washington D.C., but she eventually moved to New York City and married Johnny Jones. They adopted a baby boy, named Johnny. Laura died in 1955, and both her husband and son have since passed.

THE RICHARD DAVIS FAMILY IN CALLANDS

As I grew up, I gradually became aware of uncles, aunts and first cousins on Daddy's side, but there were many more Davises I didn't know about. I used to hear Daddy, Esther and Sallie refer to certain people as our kinfolk, but their exact relationship was never explained, or I was not listening carefully enough.

Joe Henry's brother, Richard Davis, was the oldest sibling, and he was born 1848. His wife, Martha, was probably born in 1857. Records indicate that they had 8 children: Leonard Son Davis, Flunory Risk Davis, Caroline Sim Davis, Florence Davis, Mary Davis, Lillie Bell Davis, Jenny Davis and Lucinda Davis. They were raised in Pittsylvania County, Virginia.

Daddy often spoke about his cousins, Spencer and Henry Davis, who he said were so light that they could "pass for white." In fact, he said that Spencer would deliberately hang around the whites sometimes and tell his relatives what they said. Their parents were Leonard (Son) Davis and Susie Wright; and their other siblings were Viola, Leonard Jr., Acie, Monroe, Richard and Virginia. They lived in the Callands community on Flint Hill Road.

Flunory (Risk) Davis, Leonard's younger brother, was married to Thelm Wright. They had 4 children: Daisy Bell, Harry, Phillis and Flunory Jr. They also lived in Callands.

James Davis, Joe Henry's other brother, was married to Mattie, and according to nephew Roy Banks Breedlove, James moved to Yanceyville or Reidsville, North Carolina. Their 6 children were Jim Orange Davis, Viola Davis, Uniecy Niecy Davis, Golden Davis, Evelenia Ting Davis and Helen Davis. (So far, I haven't met anyone from this wing of the family).

Emma and Sallie were Joe Henry's sisters. Emma Davis was married to Booker Breedlove, and they had 6 children: James, Richard, Roy (Banks), Joe, Willie and Evelyna. The lived in the Tunstall District. Sallie Davis married William Emmus Griggs, and they had 9 children: John Henry, Eddie Boyd, Joseph, William, Fannie, Mamie, Emily and Elizabeth. They also lived in the Tunstall District.

During my visits with my Aunt Sally Ramsey and Aunt Esther Early, I learned about my grandfather's siblings. When I was in Washington, D.C. I met Mamie Griggs Davis, who lived in Maryland. Aunt Esther told me that we were related to the Breedloves, and she introduced me to Vincent and Mary Ann Breedlove and their son Vincent Jr. (whom she took care of while Mary Ann worked). They lived in Hampton, Virginia, where I was attending Hampton University.

My father always spoke highly of Roy Banks Breedlove, and he took us to see him when we were younger. However, during those days I was not motivated to find out more about our kinship. Fortunately, I was able to visit Banks Breedlove at his home in Dry Fork on the occasion of his 100th birthday, at which time I leaned in to listen to his account of our extended family.

Also present at that occasion were Mr. Breedlove's wife and daughters. Evelyna, the youngest daughter, was married to Rev. Ross, and she was the executive director of the PCCA (Pittsylvania County Community Action Agency). She also has been elected vice president of the County NAACP Branch in Chatham.

JOE HENRY DAVIS, MY GRANDFATHER (1863-1935)

I was born in 1938, 3 years after my grandfather died. What I am writing here is based mainly on what others have told me about Joe Henry. Even though he was obviously a man of considerable stature in Chatham, there is little written information about him or his work. The family Bible and other papers that existed were lost in the 1981 fire that destroyed the family house on SR 703.

My Aunt Jenny was the first person I recall commenting on Joe Henry, whom she referred to as "Brother Davis." She said Joe Henry preached at St. John's Baptist Church at a revival. I don't recall if Aunt Jenny said his wife, Linda, was with him, and I don't know what year it was; but she said that he preached a powerful sermon that drew lots of "Amens."

She also said that he was not a person to mince his words. He spoke frankly, and he occasionally used profanity and "earthy language." Like most preachers, he admonished his congregation about their sins. To the women in the front row pews, he would warn, "Don't sit up here, showing your underwear." To the men, he advised them to treat their "wives and children kindly, and make sure they attend church and follow the teachings of the Bible." He did not approve of excessive drinking and drunkenness.

Aunt Jenny said that he was a good husband who helped his wife with household chores and with canning food for the winter months. He was a hands-on farmer, planting tobacco as his cash crop, as well as wheat, corn, beans, squash, pumpkins, sweet potatoes, tomatoes and other vegetables. He had peach, apple, pear, cherry and persimmon trees—some of which are still producing. He raised hogs, chickens, and he had a milking cow, horses and mules.

Daddy said it took "Papa" all day to deliver a load of cured tobacco to the warehouse in Danville; but he usually bought some candy or sweets for the kids. Because he was a preacher, Joe Henry attended most of the

Baptist church association gatherings. Those were both religious and social get-togethers, which involved all church members and their families who could attend.

The women brought home-cooked meals and desserts and enjoyed those opportunities to meet and greet other folks from county towns. The preachers, deacons and other important church dignitaries were recognized, and Daddy said "Papa" was always one of the preachers to be asked to deliver the opening prayer or benediction.

Joe Henry was also adept at telling stories and jokes, which Daddy shared with us, like the one about a man who outran a quarter horse to show that he should be hired. Then there was the story about a man trying to outrun a ghost, or the reaction of a preacher giving a eulogy when the body in the open casket suddenly sat up.

The photos we have of Joe Henry Davis and Linda Craft Davis show them to be a very handsome couple. He was quite fair, with fine hair and keen features. He was of average height (5' 10") and well-built. Gramma Linda was also fair in complexion and had reddish hair that was coarser. She and Aunt Jenny looked very much alike. From the photos, she looks more thoughtful and serious than happy.

Joe Henry was born in 1863 as slavery was coming to its dramatic and violent end during the bloody Civil War. It is not clear exactly where he was born, but court and tax records indicate that he more than likely grew up in the southwestern part of Pittsylvania County, or Henry County.

The town of Axton, about 15 miles west of Danville, is home to a lot of Davises, who are relatives of one degree or another. Tax records I have indicate that he paid taxes in the Tunstall District in the 1880s and 1890s. He raised tobacco, like most farmers. Some of his brothers and sisters lived in the immediate area and in nearby Dry Fork.

Joe Henry's parents, Joe Davis and Jane (Carter) Davis, are listed in Pittsylvania County court marriage records in 1882. Records indicate that they were also the parents of Richard Davis, James Davis, Emma (Davis) Breedlove, and Sally (Davis) Griggs. So far, I have been unable to find their burial site.

THE CRAFTS AND OTHER RELATIVES IN NEW JERSEY

My hometown, Scotch Plains, New Jersey, or more specifically, "Jerseyland," was a community where other families with roots in Pittsylvania County, Virginia, had settled. The Lipfords, Womacks and Pruntys were from southside Virginia. Relatives told me that we were related to the Pruntys, and I remember "cousin" Carrie Prunty and her sons, who lived on Jerusalem Road. Daddy often stopped to visit them and Mrs. Pugh, who lived next door.

Another family we were related to, the Smiths, also lived in Jerseyland. Sunny and Fannie Smith had at least 8 children, and they lived on Turney Avenue. Sunny was short, thin and of light complexion. Fannie was also fair, but of a heavier build. Both had fine, dark wavy hair, as did their children. The oldest child, Trottley, could pass for white, but the other siblings were accurately described as "mulattoes," or Indians. There was Dudley, Ezekiel, Kelsey, Otha, Quella, Luella and Aleece. They were all much older than me, but I do remember some of them.

Ezekiel was known for shooting a cigarette from his brother's mouth with a 22. Rifle. Trottley was said to hold a younger brother over the well by his ankles and drop and then catch him. The last time I saw Trottley was when he came back home and stopped by to see my father in the 1950s. He was living in Missouri. Dudley worked with Daddy and me clearing a wood lot in Scotch Plains on Front Street. He built a house on Smith Street, next to the Community Center. When I was in high school, I met Lorlei Adams, and for a time we hung out together. She was the daughter of Quella and Tee Adams.

When I retired and moved to Chatham in 2000, I discovered a letter that Fannie Smith wrote to her husband, Sunny. It was postmarked from Gretna, Virginia. Apparently, this letter was in my Aunt Jenny's papers, which my father retained after she died in 1960. Quella and Tee Adams came down to spend time with my parents in Chatham after Daddy retired and moved back home.

There was an older lady named Angeline Craft who lived near us on Plainfield Avenue in Scotch Plains. I remember looking after her, running errands and keeping her company. I never knew her husband, but I remember well her adopted son Harold, his wife Amelia, and their children, Janet, Harold, and Connie.

Once when I was being a jerk, teasing Connie, Harold Sr., a special policeman, handcuffed me to the bedpost, and I stayed there until he came home from work. Amelia died, and Harold remarried and moved to Keyport, New Jersey, where he found employment as a chef. Harold Jr. became a tour bus driver and occasionally stopped by to visit old friends and family in Jerseyland.

Jim and Susie Craft and their sons, Richard and Howard, lived in Plainfield on Cottage Street. Daddy told us how they were forced to flee from their home in Chatham when they were threatened by racists who wanted their farm. According to Daddy, there were some white men who claimed that Jim's deed to his farm was illegitimate, and they tried to run him and Susie off their land. When Jim complained to the county sheriff, the sheriff replied that he would have to "protect himself."

Consequently, he and Susie did just that, resulting in a shoot-out one night on their property. When it was over, a few white men were shot, and under the cover of night, Jim and Susie rode into Chatham and caught the 2 a.m. train heading north. They eventually settled safely in Plainfield, New Jersey. I am sure they were related to my grandmother, Linda Craft, or to the Davises in Chatham. I remember visiting them in Plainfield with Daddy.

I had heard the story of one Jack Craft, who lived in the mountains near Beckley, West Virginia. He was related to my grandmother Linda's family who lived in that area. Daddy described him as an outlaw who committed robbery and hid out in the mountains. He wore a pair of 32/20 pistols and would not hesitate to use them.

Daddy recalled those stories with obvious relish, because he was proud of how those men stood up to the racist establishment. He also told us about an "Uncle Jim," who had been a slave and who apparently was brave and smart enough to sneak around the county to visit other slaves, in violation of his master's rules. He somehow got someone to write out a pass or a letter of permission from his master, which he used occasionally.

Our family's experience with another relative was not so positive. In the post WWII period, 1947-1953, one relative came to stay with us in Scotch Plains for a while. He was supposed to be looking for employment, but he discovered where Daddy kept his savings locked up, and he stole about $1,000.00 and fled.

I was too young to remember much about him, but I do know he was a charmer, like con men tend to be. Daddy never recovered his hard-earned savings, despite the young man's father promising to return the money. This experience made my father suspicious of anyone coming into our house, or of us "bothering" any of his personal things.

I can still see the desk at the top of the stairs where the money was stored with the padlock, which had been pried loose with a claw hammer. Daddy may not have reported the theft, hoping that the money would be returned. I don't know whether Daddy ever heard from that relative again.

THE MINORS, THE MUSES AND THE STEWARTS

My mother, Gertrude Minor, was one of 7 children born to Florida Minor in the small town of Cumnor, in King and Queen County, Virginia. Florida apparently worked for a white family who owned a store and adjoining land. She stayed in the back of the store. Two of her children were fathered by the son of her employer. Momma and her sister Ivory were light-skinned and had long fine dark hair, while all the other siblings were dark with coarse hair.

Momma always felt a degree of shame about her mother's circumstance, and about how it affected her relationship with her brothers and sisters.

Robert Minor, the oldest child, came to stay with us in Scotch Plains in 1953. He and his family lived in South Jersey, and he was looking for work in construction. I remember him more clearly, especially his manner of speaking and the stories of his youth in Virginia.

When his mother died, he was taken in by a man who was very strict and cruel. When he did anything wrong, he was hung up by his wrists and whipped by this man, who was a relative. Eventually, Robert ran away and made a life for himself. He and his wife had several children while living in South Jersey. Their twin girls kept in touch with my mother, and after she passed, I spoke with one on the phone, who lived in Boston.

Momma's older sister, Winnie, with whom she was close, was married to David Muse, who was also from King and Queen County, Virginia. They had two children, Roosevelt and Alberta, and they lived in Westfield, New Jersey. Uncle David was a kind man who I remember took the time to spend with us kids, making us feel welcome. Unfortunately, he died too early. Aunt Winnie, who learned to drive and always had her own car, often traveled back to Virginia to see the folks who raised her and spent time with me, my siblings and our children at family gatherings. She lived to the age of 92.

Reginald Minor was another brother. He moved up to Philadelphia and served in the military during WWII. I never had any contact with him. He was 95 when he died. Edward Minor was younger than Momma, and he also lived in Philadelphia. He came over to visit us on several occasions, and he and Momma corresponded regularly. He was a handyman, a cabinet-maker and a good cook. On the last occasion he visited us in Scotch Plains, he brought his lady friend.

Thomas Minor (Bagby) was also younger than Momma. He lived in Petersburg, Virginia, and had a daughter I never met. He came to visit Momma and Daddy in Chatham once before Daddy died, and he came to Daddy's funeral. The last visit he made was in 2001, but he was very frail then. We were not notified of his passing.

Ivory Minor was older than Momma, and she also lived in the Philadelphia area. She had children, but I don't know anything about them. She enjoyed life but also died too soon.

Ella Minor was the youngest sibling. She was living in Cumnor and working. She and Momma corresponded often, and I found some of her letters after Momma died. Daddy took us to Bordentown to visit Cousin

Nancy a few times. She lived in her own home with her husband and son. She kept a neat house, was a stickler for cleanliness and her yard had flowers and grapes. She did domestic work for white families. Her husband was disabled and didn't work outside of the home.

Momma said that before she went to live with Cousin Nancy, she was staying with another relative and his wife and son. One day, she and the boy were cutting wood with an axe—instead of the saw—which made the patriarch of the family angry. He began whipping Momma with a big switch because she had disobeyed him. He hit her on the head several times, drawing blood, until his wife screamed at him to stop. After such treatment, she was happy to go home with Nancy Stewart.

When my mom first arrived at her cousin's home in Bordentown after her attack in her previous residence, she faced resentment and jealously for the attention she received from her cousin's son, which included a time when he hit her on the head with a stick or a blunt object, re-opening an old wound that caused a lifelong sore spot. Fortunately, they eventually learned to get along.

As a devout Christian, Cousin Nancy regularly attended church, and she was a no-nonsense person. She moved quickly and spoke clearly and meant what she said. Momma loved her and always felt beholden to her.

When I started driving in 1955, I took Momma, Lorraine and JoAnn to visit the Stewarts in Bordentown. When I graduated from Hampton University in 1961, I stopped in Bordentown for an overnight with the Stewarts. With my car was loaded down with luggage and ceramics, I needed a rest. Cousin Nancy was thrilled that I was going to Liberia, West Africa, to teach. The last time I visited them was after I got married in 1965-66.

ESTHER AND FERD EARLY
AND THE BREEDLOVES IN HAMPTON, VIRGINIA

After I graduated from high school in 1957, I decided to attend Hampton University in Hampton, Virginia. My decision was influenced by my Aunt Esther and her husband, Ferd Early, who lived there. They spoke highly of the school and encouraged me to come down for a visit. My brother Joe drove us down in his brand new 1956 Ford, and we had a great time touring the campus, including Fort Monroe, where Ferd worked, and Langley Air Force Base

I'm glad I had the chance to live in a community of educated Black people, where I was happier than I would have been if I had chosen to attend Rutgers. I enjoyed the comfort of Aunt Esther's home, even though

I lived on campus. I made the right decision, spending 4 of the happiest years of my life at Hampton, right on the Chesapeake Bay.

Aunt Esther was Daddy's oldest sister, which I didn't know at that time. He had spent time with her in Uniontown, Pennsylvania, when she was married to Charlie Tarpley. She valued education and was proud of the time she attended Ingleside Seminary. Strong-willed, she was domineering and a very devout Christian who, like her siblings, was easily excitable and emotional. On the home front, she was an excellent housekeeper, a good cook and hostess. She and Ferd were raising their grandson, who suffered from a cleft palate, which required several surgeries that they paid for.

Esther had two sons by her first husband: Bill, and Jimmy. They grew up in Uniontown, but they had moved to the Tidewater area after time in the Army. Bill was married to Claire, and they had 4 children: Martel, Barbara, Sharon and Richard. Jimmy and wife, Lorraine, moved to New Port News with their son, Charles. I spent time with both families during my time at Hampton.

Bill worked in the Post Office in Hampton and was an accomplished artist. He spent time at Hampton University's Art department, painting in watercolors and oil, and he was also a pottery buff. I have one of his oil paintings in my house now. He became an ordained Minister later in life. At my father's funeral in 1983, Bill offered a moving eulogy. He and Claire still reside at their home on Elm St in Hampton.

Uncle Ferd was a carpenter/cabinetmaker by trade and was a federal employee at Fort Monroe, with a daughter from a previous marriage. A jovial, friendly, happy man, he was always fun to be around. As a youth during the Great Depression, he was a hobo for a time, traveling across the country. Thus, he had a lot of tales to share, such as his explanation about how he started chewing tobacco when he met a girl in Tennessee who he later discovered dipped snuff. He said he decided to try it himself to get close to her!

When Esther and Ferd moved to Hampton after WWII, they rented an apartment at Dr. McCallister's house on King Street. He was the school dentist at Hampton. When they could afford it, they purchased their own house on nearby Union Street. It was beautifully furnished, and Esther kept it clean and neat inside. Their yard had many pretty flowers, a neatly mowed lawn, and in the rear was Ferd's shop.

He drove a Plymouth, but Esther did not drive (except from the back seat!). After I left Hampton, a gentrification project caused all the Union Street houses to be demolished, to be replaced by a housing project. Ferd and Esther then bought a nice ranch-style house on New Port News Avenue.

Aunt Esther broadened my knowledge of our relatives. She spoke a lot about "Papa" and her siblings. She told me how hard Daddy worked as a boy, plowing with the mules. "Papa" would tell young George in jest, "Boy take it easy on those mules. Put them in the shade for a spell." She also said that "Papa" and "Momma" were strict on her, Sally and Laura. Local boys knew they had to step lightly and show a proper reverence and respect when they came to visit.

Esther told me about the Breedloves in Chatham, and she introduced me to Vincent and Mary Ann Breedlove, who lived in Hampton. She took care of their little son, Vince Jr., while Mary Ann worked. It was never clear how closely we were related, but I suppose I didn't ask enough questions at the time. The last time I saw them was at Esther's funeral in Hampton, in 1985. Ferd preceded her in death.

GERALD, GALE AND CHANNING DAVIS:
CHATHAM RESIDENTS

I retired from teaching at Northfield Mount Hermon School in June 2000. After 3-plus decades at that wonderful school, Gale and I were ready to move on to the next chapter of our lives. Our oldest son Channing, who had been working in the dining Hall at NMH, moved with us. His brother, Sterling, who graduated from NMH and Emerson College, was working in Hollywood, California, at the American Film Institute. He is a photographer, graphic designer, and he works on various TV shows as an editor.

One of the reasons I wanted to relocate to Chatham was to be near Momma, who was 87 and living independently in the nice single-wide my father purchased in 1976 when he retired. I drove him and my sister JoAnn to Chatham, where Daddy met his lawyer to finalize his deed and arrange for the upcoming move. Daddy bought a beautifully equipped Oakwood home, fully furnished and ready to move in. My brother Joe and his wife Shirley accompanied them on their trip south. Daddy's big Dodge station wagon was overloaded, resulting in flat tires and other problems, but they made it safely.

Gale, the boys and I enjoyed our annual trips south, stopping in Chatham for a few days before driving on down to Columbus, Georgia, to see Gale's family. Daddy walked us around the property, down through the low grounds, pointing out who our neighbors were. Though his health was failing, he made some improvements on the property.

He cleared a space for a garden down by the spring and created a small pool by blocking up the creek. It was a nice place to sit during the heat of the day. Since he stopped his brother from cutting pulpwood, the trees had grown considerably, except for on the tobacco fields he leased out to Giles, a farmer who lived nearby. The money he gained from the lease was practically enough to cover the annual tax bill.

From 1976 until Daddy died in August 1983, he and Momma entertained family and friends who visited. Acie Dan, his wife Mary, Acie Jr. and his wife Mable and their children had been living in the old house, until Acie Jr. bought a trailer in 1976. After the house burned down in 1981, Acie Dan and Mary moved in with Acie Jr. and Mable. All that remained of the house were the two big chimneys. Daddy was very upset over the loss of the old homestead.

Acie and Mary's other children, Clara Jean, Delores, Mariah, Lillian Ann, Shirley and Katie were married or living elsewhere in the county. Anne, her husband, Leonard Craft, and son, Darius, lived in Gretna. Delores and her husband, Connie, and daughters lived in Penhook; Mariah got married and had several children. Shirley had a daughter, JoAnn. Katie, and the youngest had a daughter, Krystal, and she eventually married P. L. Leftwich of Whitmell. Clara, the oldest, was married to Leonard Adkins, and they lived in Danville. They had children, but I don't know their names.

I am sorry that I never had the opportunity to get to know Delores as an adult. I learned that she suffered a tragic loss when her daughter died in a house fire in Penhook. She never quite got over the accident. Her husband, Connie, was a logger who died in a workplace accident.

BUYING A HOME AND MOVING

We had never purchased a house, because we lived at a school that provided us with free housing and meals. Since 1973, we were living in a nice brick house with a two-car garage and full basement on campus. So we had so much stuff to dispose of and pack up for the move.

Fortunately, we found ABF who provided a 28-foot. trailer which we loaded. They picked it up and drove it to our new home, a 28 x 60-foot Fleetwood double-wide on the family property in Chatham. We actually arrived in Chatham on the 1st of July 2000, after an overnight in Silver Spring, Maryland, with Gale's sister, Rosalind. I drove my Ford F-150 truck, loaded down, while Channing drove our '92 Honda Accord with Gale.

My brothers, Joe and Danny, were in Chatham when the ABF truck arrived, so they helped us unload the trailer. The home had been here since 1995, but it was unfurnished, except for two beds and a couple chairs. The kitchen had a refrigerator and stove, and we soon bought a washer/dryer.

We had been staying here during our visits since it was set up. It was great having central air. I built a 10 x10-foot deck in the front, and later another one in the back, with a roof. Channing and I built a 12 x16-foot shed to house our tools and other items, and we eventually we put up another shed, with Joe's help, to hold our riding mower and other lawn tools.

Joe had a Jim Walters home built on the same lot where the old house stood. He knocked down the chimneys and cleared away the debris, and the house was 60 percent completed by 1991. He finished the interior with help from friends in New Jersey and from family members.

Channing and I helped with hanging sheet rock and with the foundation. He had not moved there, but he came down to work on the house and spend time with Momma. After Gale, Channing and I moved, he began to spend more time here.

By 2002, he had become a permanent resident. His wife, Shirley, remained in Plainfield, New Jersey, but she came down to visit. Joe drove back regularly to see Shirley and their children.

MEETING PEOPLE AND LEARNING THE ENVIRONMENT

Since Momma didn't drive or have a car, she spent most of her time at home. Mable took her shopping for groceries, and Milo Simmons and his sister, Hannah Fuller, also included her on their trips to Chatham or Danville. Hannah was in her 90s, but she was living alone in her home on Concord Road. Milo, a few years younger, also lived on the Simmons' farm in his own trailer.

I recall walking with Momma and our two boys to visit Hannah and her brothers, Richard, and Milo, in the 1980s. Richard was about 95, but he was spry and opinionated. He criticized Acie Dan for not taking better advantage of his opportunity. Richard owned a 1959 Chevy pickup, which he kept in the garage.

Since he stopped driving, the truck was seldom used, and eventually, after he passed, Milo tried to sell it. He had a 1955 Ford sedan which he kept in running order. Hannah's other sisters lived in Pennsylvania and Washington, D.C. Doris, the one who lived in D.C., built a beautiful brick house, across the street from Hannah. She was a good friend of Aunt Sally.

WILMER AND MARY FITZGERALD FAMILY

Mr. Wilmer Fitzgerald stopped by our house for a visit one Sunday afternoon in the summer of 2000. He and his wife, Mary, were old friends of my father. Wilmer was a tobacco farmer who owned over 100 acres on Route 57. He raised a crop of tobacco on our land and paid Daddy $400.

Mary's maiden name was "Price," and two of her brothers were Clarence and Carl, Daddy's childhood buddies. He told me how he gave Mary his coat one winter day because she didn't have one walking home from the schoolhouse.

As a moral to the story, Mary called Daddy in 1959 to let him know that our homestead was to be auctioned off because of unpaid taxes. Consequently, as mentioned before, Daddy and Joe rushed down there and stopped the auction. Even though, he shared ownership of the farm with his siblings, Acie Dan, Sallie, Esther and Laura—Daddy was the steward of the property and paid the taxes, and he later became sole owner.

Wilmer and Mary lived in a nice two-story white house on Route 57. They had 8 children: Florence, Wilmer Jr. (Young), Lee, Allan, Aubrey, Doris, Faye and Phillis. I became acquainted with them through time spent in Washington D.C. with Aunt Sally and Uncle Shirley Ramsey.

Their daughter, Linda, married Young, who was an Army Lieutenant stationed near D.C. He graduated from Virginia State College and its ROTC program, and he endured two tours in Vietnam. He was the one I mentioned switching places with so that he could join his bride at the hotel. While in the barracks, I was dumped from the bunk by his buddies in the middle of the night who thought I was him.

Linda and Young had 4 daughters: Cherie, Cherae, Cherelle and Chantell. Like other "military brats," they experienced growing up in several different environments, including South Korea, Italy, Japan, Germany and the U.S. Their permanent home was in Oxen Hill, Maryland. All graduated from college, married, had children and settled in the D.C./Virginia area.

Young retired as a Lt. Colonel, and he was employed by the Scientific and Commercial systems Corporation (SCSC) as division director of Fabrication and Assembly, and he was promoted to vice president of that Division in Falls Church, VA. He and Linda were generous hosts to extended family and friends over the years. Before he died in April 2003, he and Linda were actively planning to build a new home in Chatham. His mother, Mary, had passed, but his father was still living on his farm.

Young was buried in our family cemetery on Irish Road, behind my house. Also resting there are his brother-in-law, David Ramsey, Aunt Sallie and Uncle Shirley Ramsey. Aubrey Fitzgerald Jones, Doris Fitzgerald, and Phillis Fitzgerald Winston have since moved back home to Chatham and regularly visit their brother's gravesite. Doris took care of her father, Wilmer Sr., at her home on Main Street until his passing in 2008 at age 100.

ROY BANKS BREEDLOVE AND FAMILY

One of Daddy's childhood friends whom he talked about often was a man he called "Banks." On our trip to Chatham in 1976, we visited Roy (Banks) and Lucy Breedlove at their home in Dry Fork. I recall Banks telling the story of a young doctor whose father took a vacation and left him to care for his patients. When his father returned, the son told him how he had cured an old lady. His father was upset and told him that it was "patients like her" who had paid his way through medical school.

Banks' sight was beginning to fail him, but he continued to do what chores he could around the house. Lucy was quiet, but she was a pleasant host to us. At that time, I didn't know specifically how we were related to Roy Breedlove.

I later learned that Banks' mother, Emma, was Joe Henry's sister. She was fair in complexion with dark, wavy hair. Her husband, Booker Breedlove, was a handsome man of average height with a dark complexion. Their other children were Willie, Evelyna and James.

Banks and Lucy had two daughters: Lillie Kate Breedlove and Evelyna Breedlove Ross. Evelyna and her husband, Larry Ross, live next door to the house Banks and Lucy lived on SR 703. Larry Ross is the pastor at Rosebud Church in Chatham. Evelyna works for the County Community Action Committee and is the vice president of the county NAACP. I met her sister, Lillie, in 2006 at the Breedlove home at a family gathering. She lives in Forestville, Maryland.

When Roy Banks Breedlove turned 100, his family and friends had a big celebration party. I did not attend the affair, but Gale, Channing and I joined some others on a visit to the Breedlove home. Linda Fitzgerald, Aubrey Jones, Ronald Davis, my brother Joe, Walter Breedlove and Bank's daughters were there.

Banks sat in his recliner, but he spoke with us, answering questions about our genealogy. He was practically blind at that point. His family put together a nice color brochure with photos and short bio sketches. When Banks died in August 2007, the local media published articles about him, and CRISIS magazine, the NAACP publication, followed up with a nice complementary piece.

Banks' daughters and other family members established a scholarship fund in his name for a deserving high school graduate. Though he never finished high school, Banks insisted that his daughters go to college. He was well-known in the community for his support to those young people who were trying to get an education. His daughter, Evelyna, said that "despite the problems he encountered, like losing an eye in an accident while a boy and suffering from racial discrimination," he maintained an optimism that all who knew him recognized and saw as inspiration.

SALLY JANE DAVIS AND WILLIAM EMMUS GRIGGS

During the times I spent with Aunt Sally and Uncle Shirley Ramsey in Washington D.C., I met "Cousin" Mamie (Griggs) Davis, who lived in Silver Spring, Maryland. She had a son named Ronald, who was 4 years older than me. I only learned of how we were related when I began to research our family genealogy.

I'm not sure when I last saw Mamie, but it was probably at a funeral in Chatham. She survived her sister, Emily Griggs Adams, and probably attended the latter's funeral. Emily left her home on Mt. Cross Road near Danville. Ronald Davis had to come down from D.C. on a couple of occasions to arrange for repairs to the property. He stopped by my house on one of these visits, but I was asleep, having been up all night on the job. Ronald died on May 4, 2010, in Washington D.C. He was survived by two children, Donna and Ryan, but was predeceased by his wife. I never met his wife or children.

Emily Griggs married Samuel Adams in 1935. They raised Mary Elizabeth Burks, daughter of Daniel and Delsia Adams. Sam was a member of Piney Grove Primitive Baptist Church. He worked at Dan River Mills, Danville, for 40 years, and was known for his skills as a hunter. Emily was a member of Holbrook Street Presbyterian Church United, and a domestic worker. Samuel died in 1989 and Emily died in 2005, at 93. I never met them, but found this information in "Family Wisdom," (2006) written by Howard G. Adams, PH. D.

William Howard Taft Griggs (son of Sally Jane) and wife Martha, had two children: William Gerald and Donna. William (married Marva), and they had two children, Anthony and Katrina.

Anthony was born on February 12, 1960, in Lawton, Ohio. As a professional football player, he was a linebacker with the Philadelphia Eagles (1982-85) and the Cleveland Browns (1986-88). His NFL career began as a fourth-round draft pick for the Eagles in 1982, out of Ohio State. However, he graduated with a B.A. degree in Communications from Villanova in 1983.

After his playing career was over, Anthony joined the Pittsburgh Steelers in 1992 to work in player programs. His responsibilities included continuing education, internships, investment information and counseling services for players. He also assisted the conditioning coordinator with strength programs for players. He is married with two children. This information on the Griggs family is attributed to an unpublished genealogy on the Davis/Carter family of Pittsylvania County, Virginia.

APPENDIX

KEY DEFINITIONS AND TERMS

AFRIKANERS — The white ethnic group in South Africa descended from the early Dutch settlers in the Cape of Good Hope who eventually dominated the political system and imposed the policy of Apartheid or racial segregation on the population.

AMERICO-LIBERIANS — Liberians of African American descent who trace their ancestry to free born formerly enslaved African Americans who immigrated to Liberia in the early 19th century. They dominated the economic and political institutions in the country.

CUBAN MISSILE CRISIS — The October 1962 nuclear missile scare between the U.S. and the Soviet Union due to Soviet missiles in Cuba.

W. E. B. DUBOIS — An African American educator, publicist and one of the founders of the NAACP, the National Association for the Advancement of Colored People.

MARCUS GARVEY — A Jamaican political activist, businessman, and orator who founded the Universal Negro Improvement Association, 1914, and declared himself "Provisional President of Africa."

ALTHEA GIBSON — The first African American female winner of the Wimbledon Tennis championship in 1956.

BILLY GRAHAM — An American evangelist and ordained Southern Baptist minister who became internationally famous in the 1950s and 1960s for the revivals held in several countries.

"DADDY KING" — Reverend Martin Luther King, Sr., the father of Martin Luther King, Jr., the famous civil rights leader, and president of The Southern Christian Leadership Conference.

L A M C O — Liberian American Mining Company that was building the railroad from the iron ore mines to the coast.

i

KPELLE — One of the largest tribal groups in the Central Province of Liberia.

KWE QUELLI — A word in the Kpelle language that refers to a white person and or an educated foreigner.

JOE LOUIS — An African American professional boxer, and heavy weight champion, 1934- 1951; considered the greatest heavy weight boxer of his era, affectionately dubbed "the Brown Bomber".

KWAME NKRUMAH — The first African prime minister of Ghana, the first
British West African colony granted independence, 1957.

PLEBEIANS — The main body of free Roman citizens who were not Patricians, referred to as "commoners."

TEDDY RHODES — An African American professional golfer who helped break the color barrier in the PGA, Professional Golf Association.

CHARLIE SIFFORD — The first African American professional golfer to play on the PGA tour, winning the Greater Hartford Open in 1967.

EMETT TILL — A 14-year-old African American who was brutally tortured and lynched in Mississippi in 1955 after being accused of offending a white female store clerk.

SEKOU TOURE — The first African president of the French West African colony, Guinea, 1958.

NAT TURNER — black man who led the only "effective, sustained slave rebellion" in U.S. history in 1831 in the state of Virginia.

USAID — United States Agency for International Development which distributed American economic assistance to African and other developing countries.

BOOKER T. WASHINGTON — An African American educator, founder and president of Tuskegee Institute, Alabama, and leading 19th century African American spokesman.

ROY WILKINS — A prominent African American civil rights activist and NAACP Secretary in the 1930s. He remained active in the civil rights movement from 1934 to the late 1970s.

WHITNEY YOUNG — An African American civil rights leader and social worker and president of the National Urban League, 1961-1971.